"Your ability to understand and select good commercial real estate can make you rich, and this book shows you better than any book you'll ever read." –**Brian Tracy, Speaker, Author, Consultant**

"Whether you're a real estate novice or an experienced pro wanting to dramatically improve your performance, *Pure Profits* deserves very careful reading and total digestion. There's no question that this book will help you either get started right or finally get it right afterwards." –**Dr. Joseph E. McCann, Dean, The University of Tampa**

"Al Auger is the quintessential real estate professional who employs the three P's: Persistence, Practicality, and the often overlooked ingredient for any successful relationship, Personality. I have witnessed his refined techniques firsthand with the Auto Nation rollout and our own real estate developments. They work, and they will help you be more successful!" –**Jim Hendrix, Vice President, Land Acquisitions & Development, Continental Real Estate Company**

"Bravo! You couldn't have presented a more logical approach for getting started in commercial real estate investing. After almost twenty years in buying commercial real estate for various corporations, I have finally found a great reference book for the real estate professional. If you were looking for a mentor and for guidance, *Pure Profits* is all you need." –**Alex Dominguez, MCR, CCIM, Sr. Director of Real Estate, Chick-Fil-A, Inc.**

"In designing and managing investment portfolios for more than twenty-five years, I have come to appreciate the role that real estate can play in adding diversification, and hence safety, to one's net worth. There are basically only two ways to acquire real estate: one is through a public or private securities offering, and the second is doing it on your own. *Pure Profits* is a must-read for anyone who wants to do the latter!" –**Joseph F. Bert, CFP Chairman and CEO, Certified Financial Group, Inc**

"Al Auger does a great job getting to the point quickly and helping the reader understand that hard work, diligence, and common sense go a long way in a very competitive market. He clearly outlines the mechanics to enter a business in which knowledge is king." –**Robert Breslau, President, Stiles Retail Group**

"*Pure Profits* is a practical, common sense approach to commercial real estate, providing insights and information you can put into practice easily. I highly recommend this book to anyone just starting in commercial real estate, as well as to those already in the business."
–Sandra Shaver, Real Estate & Development Manager (retired), 7-Eleven, Inc.

"Kudos to Al Auger! Here is a clear and complete work that will serve as the definitive primer for those interested in acquiring skills in virtually all areas of commercial real estate. Whether you are making a career change or seeking some advanced professional knowledge, *Pure Profits* will be your most valuable resource."
–Dr. E. Backstein, DMD

"*Pure Profits* contains the simple secrets to a successful career in commercial real estate. Al explains the development process, from site selection to property management, in a concise yet thorough manner. A few hours with Al's book will save you years of trial and error. If I were just starting out in commercial real estate today, this is the one book I would choose to advise me, caution me, and support me in my career. Complete and highly readable."
–Chuck Borysiak, President, Kodiak Properties

The compass is always seeking the truth. The early explorers used the compass as their most reliable instrument for finding their direction. No matter what kind of weather they encountered along their journey, the compass helped keep them on course.

A magnetized needle that pivots freely, the compass is a valuable tool directing you through a successful journey.

Pure Profits

*Pinpoint Winning Properties,
Think Like an Investor, &
Succeed in Commercial Real Estate*

Al Auger

02 03 04 05 HH 10 9 8 7 6 5 4 3 2 1
Printed in the United States of America
ISBN: 0-9715739-3-X
Library of Congress Control #: 2002113084

Requests for permission to make copies of any part of this work can be made to:

Baron Hall, LLC
120 International Parkway #220
Heathrow, FL 32746
Phone: 1-888-709-7873
Fax: 407-804-9182

To Lori, my wife, best friend, greatest ally, and tremendous life partner. To my son Tyler, your unique and special qualities are your greatest gifts and have helped me keep it simple and real.

And to Rodeo and his mentor Two Bucks, whose tails wag in approval of anything we all do.

Contents

Contents

Foreword

I've always been a firm believer in asking questions and learning from others. This belief is what enabled me to succeed in various jobs and careers in my early years. Whenever I started in a new field, I immediately learned everything I could about the business, applied that knowledge faithfully, and ultimately attained results that surpassed others in my field.

Because of the results I achieved, I realized that I had stumbled upon an important business rule, one that I expand upon in my book *Create Your Own Future*. That rule is "If you do what other successful people do, nothing can stop you from eventually getting the same results they do. And if you don't do what they do, nothing can help you."

Al Auger is certainly one of those successful people when it comes to buying, selling, and investing in commercial real estate. Why? Because Al has consistently developed a plan of action, followed through with his plan, and has had the flexibility to make adjustments to his plan as the events transpired. By applying these principles, he has produced exceptional results faster than many people ever imagined possible. So if making money and limiting risk in commercial real estate is what you want, then Al Auger is definitely the person to learn from. In *Pure Profits*, Al helps you understand what the commercial real estate high-achievers do to attain results so you can earn more money and take complete control of your life.

Taking control is important, because when you take control, you create your future. If you're like most people, you probably want a future of health, happiness, and prosperity. But how do you attain that? How do you bridge the gap between what you *want* and what you *have,* and how do you overcome the obstacles that slow you down? The key is to learn the basics behind what you want and then practice those guidelines daily.

In *Pure Profits*, Al stresses the importance of not only learning the basics, but also mastering each basic in a "complete package," which he explains is the backbone of your investing success. In a straightforward manner, Al details the essentials to commercial real estate and gets to the heart of what you need to do to excel. He stresses the importance of setting goals, developing strong relationships, gaining knowledge, taking daily action-oriented steps, and constantly refining your skills – all of which are the business growth elements that will jump-start your future.

But mastering the business basics is only half of the equation. In addition to developing the professional aspects of yourself, your success in commercial real estate also depends on how well you develop the personal aspects of yourself. Self-development is one of those "basics" to creating your future. Al addresses this aspect as well. He gives you the tools you need to develop not only your outer wealth, but also your inner wealth – your self-esteem, your self-confidence, your interpersonal skills, and so much more. It is this kind of "complete package" that will enable you to succeed in commercial real estate, because you will only attain success in anything in life when you *believe* that you can.

The truth is that the successful commercial real estate developers, brokers and investors are those who have committed to the principles and steps Al outlines here. They are the ones who have completed the exercises, who have driven their territory, who have built their network database, and who have learned from the masters before them. As a result, they accomplish more in just a few short years of their career and/or investing objectives than others do in an entire lifetime.

Packed with solid advice and proven techniques, *Pure Profits* will help you go from being a "good" commercial real estate broker or investor to a truly great one. Al gives you the professional and personal development guidance that will enable you to overcome obstacles and that will give you unlimited opportunities to earn and learn. Even if you should walk away from this book with the decision not to pursue future commercial real estate investments, you will still come out ahead. You'll have mastered valuable business and life skills that can transcend into any future path you decide to follow.

If you have ever wanted to take the fast-track approach to investing in commercial real estate, or if you've been looking for the high-performance techniques that will move your brokerage career forward, this is the book for you. I hope that reading this book will cut years from your real estate learning curve, and that it will enable you to create the future of your dreams.

-Brian Tracy

Acknowledgments

Over the past 22 years of working in the real estate field, I have met many wonderful people and intelligent real estate investors. In that experience, I can attest to a common characteristic of the savviest investors: They came from very humble beginnings. A useful addition to my own experiences has been the knowledge that I gained from such individuals, and for that I am truly grateful.

Much like any real estate project, writing a book requires planning and preparation. Building the team to help you through the process is essential to your success. I learned that more than ever in the process of creating this book. Many people helped with this project, and to that I thank everyone.

I have grown leaps both personally and professionally. I have re-learned the fact that focus, dedication, persistence and plain hard work can get you what you want. But you cannot go it alone. I add this special thank you to my friend Renee, my unofficial "editor-in-chief," who simply understood me every step of the way. Thank you to my friend and publicist Pam Lontos for believing in the project. Thank you to Brian Tracy for your generous help and the reinforcement of the gift that we all possess – the power of achieving anything we want in life. We simply need a catalyst to get it started.

Thanks a million to Dr. Joseph E. McCann, Jim Hendrix, Alex Dominguez, Sandra Shaver, Joseph F. Bert, Robert Breslau, Dr. Ed Backstein, Mr. Kim Schwenke, and Bruce Mattson for reviewing the manuscript and offering their valuable advice. To my editor Dawn Josephson, whose fine efforts helped shape this project and bring it to life, I am sincerely grateful. I also appreciate the early work of Christine Blank for transcribing and processing the early stages of this project. I acknowledge my appreciation to Cameo Publications for their guidance and understanding in the creation of this book. Dave, I especially thank you for your patience.

Finally, to my family, Lori and Tyler, thank you for your support, your understanding, and your love. You are irresistible and tremendous human beings. I love you both.

Pure Profits ~

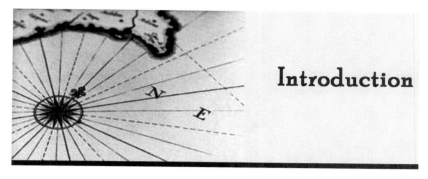

W hen I first started in the real estate business, I was struggling financially. I had little money and huge student loans to repay. Money was so tight that budgeting every penny was an absolute necessity. In order to live as frugally as possible, I ate homemade spaghetti dinners six nights a week. At $1.07 per plate, including sauce from the jar plus melted mozzarella cheese for added taste, it was a cheap meal. Despite my situation, I never lost sight of my goal – to achieve financial wealth through the buying and selling of real estate.

At that time I knew little about the actual intricacies of the real estate business and routinely heard countless horror stories about failed projects, costly bankruptcies, and bad deals. Yet all I saw was an opportunity to work in a field that would give me both personal and professional rewards. I made it a point to meet and align myself with some of the best real estate developers in the country so I could learn everything possible about achieving success in this field.

Little by little I gained hands-on knowledge, taking steps and strategies that worked in one situation and combining them with new ideas I learned during another. As the months went by, I started seeing a pattern develop and I was able to successfully close large real estate transactions. As I field-tested my new strategies, I realized that I had uncovered a step-by-step system for commercial real estate success.

The defining moment occurred one Thursday afternoon when I was driving in my car and looking at some local real estate. I turned down a dirt road when I saw it: a two-acre piece of vacant land with agricultural zoning in an industrial area. I knew in my gut that it was a prime commercial investment. The events that followed allowed me to put my buying and selling guidelines to the test.

For the next three hours I drove around the area of the property, gathering information about the surrounding vicinity. The information uncovered a gem. The property was exactly two miles from a major east-west interstate highway and one and one-half miles from a north-south interstate unlimited access highway. With that kind of accessibility to major roadways, the property was a terrific location for a company's distribution center. Comparable information obtained by contacting each of the listing agents for the surrounding properties provided me the basis for the location's financial prospects.

This property was particularly intriguing, as it was the only one without a "For Sale" sign on it. I'm a firm believer in leaving no stone unturned, so I probed a little deeper. *"Why isn't this property listed with a broker, especially since almost every other property in the area is?"* I wondered. *"Did people overlook it because it was on a dirt road?"* *"Did the county have plans to pave the dirt road?"* *"Was there something wrong with this property?"* I continued this line of questioning as the information gathering process continued.

Collecting information from the local building and zoning departments in the property's jurisdiction (detailed in chapters three) uncovered an important find. The county intended not only to pave the dirt road, but also to extend it and connect it to another road just to the north of the property, which would significantly increase people's access to the property. What a find! I knew that this one tidbit of information could translate to increased property value, provided that no one else has discovered the same information.

Map of Described Property & Vicinity:

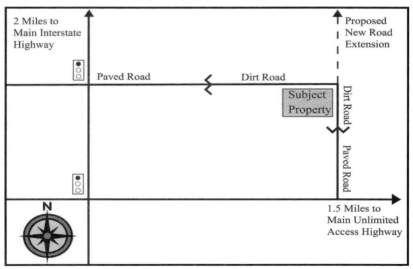

Excited about all the facts already uncovered, I thought to myself: *"I must get this property under contract as quickly as possible so I can investigate its value before someone else does."* I rushed to the local property appraiser's office, looked up the property owner, and contacted him directly. We made an appointment to meet.

My first roadblock appeared when the owner said he did not want to sell the property. His refusal only made me believe in the property more, so I requested another meeting with the property owner…and then another. My three-meeting negotiating tactic (detailed in chapter six) worked well. After the third meeting, he agreed to sell the property.

What made the difference? The owner informed me that my approach with him greatly differed from that of the hundreds of buyers and brokers who had already approached him. He explained that everyone else went on and on about how capable they and their companies were at getting property sold. But no one had taken the time to do two important steps: 1) to follow-up, and 2) to *listen* and *hear* what was really important to the property owner.

It turned out that the property had been in the man's family for many generations, and he had emotional ties with it. He couldn't bear the thought of some real estate developer coming in and changing something that had been a part of his life and heritage. To him, it would feel as if he were erasing his entire family's past.

I heard what he was saying, and I proposed an idea – name the real estate development project after the man's family. With that, the property owner agreed to sell. Now, rather than viewing the transaction as a loss of his heritage, he saw it as a living tribute to his family name. Attention to such details gave the property owner confidence in my ability to solve problems and close deals.

But getting the man to sell was just the tip of the iceberg. Now I had a larger problem to deal with: Where was I going to get the money?

By this time I had already become my own broker, so I had a good start in raising some of the required down payment money. If I could close the transaction, I could use some of my 10% real estate commission towards the financing. **(Hint for people just starting out: Get your real estate license!)** I now had to locate additional money sources.

Convincing a friend to put up the required $5,000 deposit instantly made him a partner in the project. We now had a great piece of property under contract for $135,000, yet we still needed to raise the remainder of the money to close the purchase. The pressure to perform so that my friend would not lose his deposit was huge. However, I knew I could successfully see this deal to fruition, so I put the pro forma plan together (described in chapter eight) and took action to produce a successful outcome.

After looking through my network database of investors (described in chapter two) I identified some potential targets. My first meeting with these people was stressful but successful. They asked me a lot of questions, and I answered 90% of them, promising to come back with the answers to the other 10%. After walking them through the pro forma and highlighting the major points (detailed in chapter eight) I offered the investors 80% of the project and offered my initial partner 10% of the project plus a 10% preferred return on his investment. This meant that if his $5,000 was invested for one year, he would get 10% of the profit of the entire project, plus 10% (or $500) on his $5,000. It's called a preferred return because it is paid out first. The other investors would put up the remainder of the monetary requirements above debt financing, plus their signatures. I also agreed to sign on the note. My signature was more goodwill to my investors than anything else, because I had no financial statement to back it up. The investors huddled amongst themselves to discuss my proposal.

To my surprise, they agreed to go along with the plan, subject to the following changes: They wanted to make sure that no other projects would distract me so I could stay focused on a positive outcome for this project. They also offered me an additional 15% interest in the project, reducing their interest to 65%.

"Wow," I thought. *"These guys are seasoned investors. They could have negotiated my share down to about 5% of the project."*

To me, their terms sounded like easy money…or so I thought.

I soon learned that the seasoned investors knew exactly what they were doing. They knew I would have several stressful meetings with architects, engineers, attorneys, bankers, and tenants. Then there were the lease negotiations, numerous building inspections, and plenty of delays just getting the inspectors to the project. The delays really took their toll, because all work had to stop until the inspectors approved the job. These time delays translated to money delays, because the interest on the loan kept running regardless of what happened. The delay in getting open units meant a delay in getting rental income. But no one else was worried. It seemed as if I was the only one with any sense of urgency to get this project completed in a hurry.

When the project was finally complete, I learned the final step of my process (something those investors apparently already knew): there is no such thing as a free lunch. That's right. I applied my principles and I worked and scraped for every penny I earned on that project…and it all worked out according to plan. Looking back, the fun and excitement was like winning the Olympic gold medal. I couldn't wait to repeat the process again and again. The adrenaline rush, the sense of accomplishment, and the resulting income had me hooked! The strategies behind how I actually made this seemingly impossible deal happen, from negotiating skills to money raising techniques, are detailed in this book.

What I want you to learn from this book is that for you to succeed in the real estate business, you will have to work hard and give daily application to all the techniques I teach. Yes, even the basics, such as project generation presented in chapter three, will take daily work. Why? Because if you want to be a member of that elite group of top wealth builders, you must become proficient at finding the greatest property, negotiating to get the greatest property under contract, planning your investment strategy, financing that greatest property, and most important, keeping yourself motivated and on track to closing the greatest deal of a lifetime.

(Remember: Mastery of the individual components means absolutely nothing. Achieving excellence in the complete package is what will propel you to success.)

The information and exercises in this book will help you build real wealth so you can plan for retirement, provide for your family's future, or give to a worthy cause. By picking up this program, you now have the secrets that took me twenty years to develop and that most seasoned real estate professionals still don't possess.

In addition to building wealth, the strategies in this book will help you avoid many of the pitfalls I experienced starting out. If you follow these invaluable skills, you can enjoy a higher level of professional and personal satisfaction as you quickly climb up the real estate success ladder. So grab that first rung, and let's get started.

It's time for you to stake your real estate claim.

Al

Auger

Chapter One ~

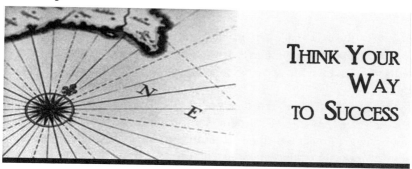

THINK YOUR WAY TO SUCCESS

Y ou have now embarked on a new venture, an undertaking that will positively change your life forever. As long as you put forth the effort and commitment, you will obtain the results you desire.

Before I continue, I must make one point perfectly clear: There is no such thing as a free lunch. Many "get-rich-quick" real estate schemes entice people with the lure of so-called "easy money." If you want real, long-lasting success, you must avoid such "programs."

In the upcoming chapters, I am going to share with you both the good and the bad of real estate buying and selling. Why the bad? Because I want to give you the complete picture so you can make your own judgments. While I want you to see how awesome real estate can be, I also want you to learn from my mistakes. I want to give you all the tools you'll ever need so you can identify the pitfalls and know how to avoid them. By keeping yourself open to new experiences and always learning from your mistakes and the mistakes of others, you can go far. That's real life.

Avoid Pitfalls & Accelerate Your Achievement

Because I entered the real estate business with no capital, I first became a real estate agent so I could receive a commission for selling properties (I cover this strategy later in the book). Taking this route enabled me to make ends meet during my early "lean" years. While becoming a real estate agent is advantageous to your outcome, it's not essential for making this process work for you. For example, if you have a current job that pays the bills adequately, you can work this program part time while you maintain your current position. As your income grows (and it will) you can then make other choices for yourself and your real estate career.

One of the first lessons I learned in this industry (which I later discovered is every successful person's foundational principle) was the importance of business ethics. Without a moral compass to guide you, any success you attain will be meaningless. In real estate, ethics translates to being true to your clients, your colleagues, and most important, yourself. Let me explain this concept in application with an example from my own past.

When I was still new to this business, I obtained a listing for a three-acre commercial property of vacant land in Florida. The listing price was $225,000, quite a lot of money twenty years ago. Once it sold, I would receive a real estate commission of anywhere from $5,625 (2.5%) to $11,250 (5%). The low/high numbers depended on whether I had a broker from another firm involved in the transaction. My goal was to sell the property quickly and make at least the minimum $5,625 commission. A few weeks later, another broker brought in the buyer. So I was looking at an automatic $5,625 payment, or so I thought.

The buyer's broker was a polite gentleman, about sixty years of age. Realizing that I was new to the business, he seemed to take on a mentoring role with me. He invited me to his home on the Intracoastal Waterway so he could share some of his experiences with me. Seeing his house motivated me and made me want to succeed in real estate more than ever before. I soon felt very comfortable with this seasoned professional.

Three days before the closing was scheduled to take place, a problem arose. I met the broker at the property for an impromptu meeting. Upon arriving at the site he said to me, "I just learned that there might be garbage buried beneath the ground. Aerial photographs dating back ten years show no such thing, so I am not convinced we have a problem, but..." His sentence trailed off, leading me to form my own conclusions. After a brief pause he continued, "I informed the buyer that we would dig some holes and check the soil condition."

He opened his car trunk, reached in for two shovels, and handed me one. Fearing that I was about to lose the deal and the $5,625 commission, I frantically started digging.

After about an hour of me digging five holes that were each five-feet-deep (compared to his solitary two-foot-deep hole), he casually strolled over to me and said, "It doesn't look like there is garbage under the soil, but I still don't know if we can get this deal closed. Let's do something that might seal the deal."

At this point I should have realized that something was not right, but the fear of losing the commission clouded my thinking. Sweat was pouring down my face, my shirt was drenched, and I looked like a puppy dog with its tongue hanging out and drooling for a biscuit.

The buyer's broker continued very calmly and in control. He said, "The buyer, who is a good friend of mine, is also a real estate broker. I think I can talk to him. He is coming to dinner tonight at my home. What can we do to really push him over the edge and close?" He paused. "It has to be something to show him that the seller really wants to sell." He paused again and looked up at the sky, scratching his chin as though he was thinking. "I know you can't reduce the purchase price. A request like that could possibly kill the deal." He paused one last time. "What do you think of this idea? We'll give the buyer 3% of the commission, I'll take 3%, and you can keep the remaining 4%."

Responding like a puppy dog that was thrown a biscuit, I leaped at the offer.

The transaction closed right on schedule. Once my mind cleared, along with the commission check, I realized what had really happened. While 4% (2% to me after my split with our firms' broker) sounded close to 2.5%, it amounted to $4,500 and resulted in the buyer getting an essential $6,750 discount on the purchase price. Was what the old man did illegal? Probably. And if he was lying about the facts, then most definitely. Nevertheless, it was a huge con job. It was also immoral and unethical behavior and absolutely not the kind of activity that will lead you to success. Beware of such unethical people and do not follow their example.

That expensive lesson 22 years ago cost me $1,125. If I could package that lesson into a textbook, some title options would be:

➢ **Desperate to close means, "Take me, I am yours."**

➢ **How to get the other party to thank you for everything you took.**

➢ **Never answer a call to dig ditches before a closing.**

➢ **The present value of $1,125, invested 20 years ago at 10%, is a steak dinner and a fish dinner for you, your spouse, and 48 other couples.**

The best way to protect yourself from these kinds of people is to know what you want out of life. When you know what you want, you are in control of your decisions and can make the best choices that are right for you. If you do not know what you want, then others will tell you what you want. And considering all the strong personalities that you will encounter in real estate, I guarantee that if you allow others to guide your choices, you will not succeed.

The key to your success is for you to be in control of your real estate projects. Then you will know what went right and what went wrong. After all, the only thing worse than a bad project is a good project in which you are unaware of the factors that made it successful.

Master the Art of Practicing Perfectly

You've surely heard the phrase, "Practice makes perfect." What's important is to make sure you're practicing the correct things. When you practice success building strategies, you will make a positive change in your life. However, if what you're practicing are counterproductive habits, then you'll never reach your full potential, no matter how hard you work.

Murphy James or "Murph," as his friends called him, exemplifies poor practicing habits. According to Murph, he had a burning desire to become a professional golfer. He started playing golf when he was five years old, and he played in his first golf tournament at age seven. He was ranked number one on his college golf team and became a club professional after graduation. However, Murph never took the final steps towards becoming a tour player.

Was Murph talented? You bet. The boy could hit any kind of golf shot on command. If the shot called for a low draw, he could hit it. If he had to hit a high fade, he would produce it on command. He was 90% down in two from the bunker.

So, what kept Murph from realizing his dream? Quite frankly, Murph didn't believe in himself. He had feelings of inadequacy. He would beat himself up over a bad shot instead of using it as a learning experience and moving on. Murph even suffered from beliefs that caused conflict in his life. He thought that to be great, he must practice, practice, and practice. So Murph practiced, all right. He practiced so much that he was tired most of the time. He practiced all his bad habits over and over again until he perfected them. Murph never took the time to learn new skills or new ways to practice. He just kept doing the same things the same way day in and day out, achieving the same poor results. Murph perfected failure in his game and in his thinking. Unfortunately, Murph failed to realize that practice *doesn't* make perfect; rather, perfect practice makes perfect.

You already possess much of the talent required to succeed at your goals. However, if you're like most people, you still need to change your habits in order to get the results you are seeking. Changing habits is a tough step, but you can do it and you are worth it. You simply need the skills and secrets in this book to lead you through the process to real wealth building. Learn new ways to work effectively so you can practice stacking one small success on top of another.

Practice "perfectly" all the strategies in these pages and do the chapter exercises. Refer to this book constantly, as it is your real estate consultant. The more you become familiar with and use the strategies in this program, the more you will gain from it. This program will ignite new thinking in you so you can devise creative strategies to reach your goals. Why is creativity important? Because real estate is a very creative business. Each project is completely different from the last and offers you a unique opportunity to learn.

Realize, too, that taking shortcuts is not the way to practice perfectly. Success in real estate requires consistency and the ability to develop a foundation of principles and teachings that you practice daily and then build upon. While many people offering "goldmine shortcuts" will tempt you, stay committed to your inner belief that you are now on the right path.

A recent lesson about the importance of consistent success building practices came in the form of a phone call from a friend of mine named Dan who was not in the real estate business, but who was intrigued by the industry and its potential financial gain. During the course of the conversation, Dan mentioned that he had responded to a real estate "educational" ad that he saw on television. In his usual excited way he told me how this program he saw advertised would teach him how to buy properties with no money down, without a credit check, and walk away from closing with $40,000 in his pocket.

Knowing the real estate industry and the truth behind those "get-rich-quick" real estate "deals," I tried to talk some sense into Dan. I explained that nothing would ever replace hard work, knowledge, artful negotiations, and the ability to raise funds. When that approach failed to make any progress, I told him about all my great banking relation-ships, and how not one of those bankers would let anyone, even me, walk away from the closing with money in my pocket, without a down payment, and with no credit.

At that, Dan began to take some notice. Not wanting my friend to make a serious mistake, I continued by explaining how there are only two ways to make money in real estate. The first way is over the long term, in which you purchase a property and wait for it to appreciate in value as the loan gets paid down. The second way is my specialty: to see something in the property that no one else sees, thereby enhancing the property's value. This enhanced value is your profit, which is often larger and comes sooner than the long-term approach.

Dan claimed to understand what I was explaining, but he felt the ad was too compelling for him not to try it. "It just seems so easy," he said.

At this, the only phrase that raced through my mind was: "If it seems too good to be true…" I think you know the rest.

Here's an update to that call: Dan is still looking for his first piece of property…and a banker who will give him such outrageous terms. My advice to you: Avoid these kinds of pitfalls and set yourself up for success.

Move From Drawbacks to Greenbacks

The lessons you will learn in this program will help you change the way you interact with people and businesses and will enhance your life over the long term. If you are looking to build real wealth, then this program will tell you how. Whatever your goal, I aim to ignite your passion to accomplish it. If you are unhappy in your current financial or business situation, then you already have the perfect catalyst for enormous change. All you need to do now is believe in yourself, learn new information and skills, commit to the program, and then constantly evaluate the results you are getting so you can make any necessary adjustments to achieve your goals.

My purpose is not to simply teach you, but also to facilitate your vision of real estate by sharing real life examples that will help you to see the "hidden value" in properties that others overlook, thereby pro-viding you the ultimate secret to huge profits in real estate. When you master the skills contained in this book you will be on a victorious jour-ney of wealth in real estate. Quite frankly, it will change your life.

Your investment in this program is really an investment in yourself. By simply picking this up, you've already proven that you are intelligent and aggressive, and that you desire new information that will take you where you want to go. As long as you believe that this course of action will take you to your destination and create the lifestyle you desire, then it will.

In the remaining chapters you will learn alternatives to the way you are currently conducting business. It's a new way of thinking that will help you examine conflicts that have prevented you from obtaining your goals in the past. Finally, you will understand how to change your beliefs in a way that will produce the best results.

You will also gain self-confidence in the mechanics of real estate. You will know what to look for and how to get it. You'll be able to answer such questions as: What makes a good property good? What makes a great investment great? How do you prepare a pro forma investment plan that is nearly impossible to say "no" to?

Because I am as dedicated to your success as you are, I consider our time together a relationship based on cooperation. By working together, we can come up with the best methods to lead you to success.

Go For The Gold!

Are you 100% committed to your successful outcome in this program? I certainly hope so. Too often, I hear people make empty promises such as, "This is the year I change my life," or "This year I will lose weight." Although these people start their new journey with unbridled enthusiasm, unlimited zest, and a seemingly solid determination, they fail consistently. How many New Years' resolutions have you successfully completed? Do you know why you failed at some yet succeeded at others? Examine each of your successes and failures. What was your commitment level during a successful project? How about during a failed project?

Ask Yourself...

☑   Are you willing to display the power, the guts, the courage, the persistence, and the commitment to follow a plan like this through to its success?

☑   Are you willing to take twenty minutes a day to get started in this business?

☑   Are you willing to increase your time commitment as you build success upon success?

☑   Are you willing to accept this plan and commit to its accomplishment, whatever it takes?

☑   Are you willing to increase your financial worth to $1,000,000 or beyond?

☑   Are you willing to close the deal of a lifetime?

Yes You Are!

Life *Is* the Vacation

Now is the time to start fresh – no more empty promises to yourself. It's time to prove your commitment. You are completely capable of doing this. You are a rare, important individual with your own goals, desires, and dreams. You are the one who has the power to make your dreams come true. I am certain your dreams are filled with fun, excitement, and success.

Remember that success is more than a vision of how you want your life to be. It's also about getting up, taking action, and making your dreams a reality. Success is about your personal enjoyment and fulfillment and about everything you can accomplish in life.

WHY ELSE WOULD YOU DO IT?

It's time to prove your commitment.

Chapter One:
Anchoring Ideas ~ An Exercise

Loosen Up
Your Real Estate
Muscles

I am not going to ask you to list your dreams and goals. Nor am I going to ask the famous self-help question: "Where do you see yourself in the next year, five years, and ten years?" That question is too hard and no one ever answers it correctly.

The dreams and goals you have are yours. You alone can picture them in your mind. You alone can feel them with your emotions. Even though most "how to" books ask for these lists, I don't. Your goals and dreams change as you move through your life, so saying that something will happen ten years from now is not productive. Flexibility is the key to goal attainment. After all, everything that you want, someone else now has. Flexibility in obtaining what you want will help you get it.

Instead...

I want you to take ten minutes and think about your commitment to this program, to your own plan of execution, to your successful mastery of the secrets, and to your completion of the wealth building exercises in this book. What are you going to do differently to achieve new results?

When you start a new physical exercise regime, you schedule the time to workout. Apply this practice to your new endeavor. Look at your day-planner and schedule the time daily for you to perform your real estate wealth building workout so that you can build a strong financial future and have fun while doing it.

Do it now. Don't procrastinate like you may have in the past. Change that habit now and take the time to think about what you are about to accomplish.

Chapter Two ~

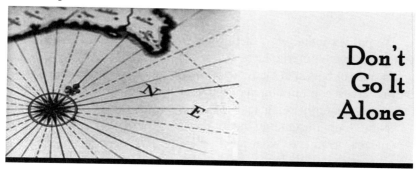

Don't Go It Alone

R eal estate is the best investment opportunity today. The facts prove it: in a recent investment survey comparing bonds, stocks, and real estate over a thirty-year period, real estate was the undisputed winner. Boasting a 12% return, real estate beat the 8% yield of bonds and the 10% return on stocks. Consistently high real estate returns are possible because real estate is a limited quantity commodity. Since no one can "make" more land, a property's value can only increase, enabling real estate to offer the best investment returns every time.

Real estate also offers the best ownership flexibility and purchasing flexibility of any investment opportunity. You can purchase property with cash, with part cash and part conventional financing, with the help of a bank or other financial institution, with a purchase money mortgage (a mortgage held by the seller of the property), or with any combination of the above. As such, virtually anyone can take advantage of a number of real estate opportunities.

Create a Broker Relationship

As you begin in your real estate adventure, you will most likely secure the services of a real estate broker to show you properties and guide you towards specific opportunities. Having a real estate broker involved with your transactions is much like a double-edged sword. The broker can be either very helpful or very hurtful to your transaction. How so? As with any profession, there are good brokers and not-so-good brokers. Regardless of whom you work with, the important thing to realize is that the broker's job is to sell the property *no matter what*, providing he or she acts ethically, morally, and within the limits of the law. Therefore, the broker is not always selling the property with your investment interests or criteria in mind.

33

To put it another way, the broker does not necessarily care about your investment criteria; he or she just wants to sell you the property – no ifs, ands or buts about it. In a way, all brokers must think this way, as they receive a commission *only* when the property sells. So in essence, the broker is simply doing a job that he or she gets paid very well to do.

Now, "notwithstanding the foregoing," (a real estate contract term that means "in spite of what I previously said"), real estate brokers are usually very helpful. Most people enjoy working with them and encourage them to present their listings. As long as you know your investment criteria well, again knowing what you want, you should be able to give the broker a fairly quick "yes" or "no" response to the submitted property. The high-quality brokers typically ask questions and attempt to ascertain your investment criteria *before* showing you any properties. This is a pre-closing technique, usually presented by their asking, *"What are your criteria so I can show you only properties that meet your investment needs?"*

Read the question carefully, because you'll notice that what it doesn't ask is: *"If I bring you a property that meets your criteria, then are you going to buy it?"* Of course, all brokers want you to purchase the first property they show you. Your job is to sort through their submissions until you find one that meets your needs precisely.

As you work with brokers, encourage them to present you all the properties they wish to show. In addition, let them know that your investment criteria are constantly changing, much like interest rates change. A good statement to use is: *"Our real estate portfolio is in constant movement."* As you sell some property types, you'll want to purchase other property types to keep your real estate portfolio diversified. Therefore, it's in the best interest of you and the broker to review a number of different properties.

The good broker is creative and will want to show you properties that may be of interest to you in the future. Be the good client and give the broker a quick indication of your interest level in each of the properties you look at. The good broker will actually listen to you and will adjust his or her offerings based on your responses.

(Hint: You will quickly learn to distinguish the good brokers from the bad brokers. If the broker calls every property he or she shows you the "best," then you'll know where that particular broker stands on the "goodness" scale. As shown later in the book, all properties are not great locations, and therefore are not great.)

As you sort through the "good" and "bad" brokers, keep an open mind and don't become "married" to any one broker. If you do, you will miss other opportunities. Here's an example:

A national corporation had asked us to find a location for them in Ohio. They needed a 25-acre site for a major retail facility. The plan was to interview two brokers in the desired city. During the interview process, each broker independently asked for an exclusive representation agreement. We respectfully denied that request in both instances. However, we did ask both brokers that they provide information on properties that they believed met our criteria as previously outlined with them. In addition, we would grant each broker exclusivity on every property presented, provided that broker could later make the transaction happen. We left each of their offices with a list of properties.

Independently, my associates and I conducted our own market studies and market analysis. The studies revealed the ideal property that neither broker had shown us. Why? The landowner simply did not work with brokers. Apparently, the brokers sensed that they would not be able to make the transaction happen with the landowner, so they omitted it from our list. They had no intention of ever showing us that particular property, even though it was by far the best property in town, adjacent to a huge regional mall.

The moral to this story is to stay single when it comes to brokers. Make it a point to identify the good and bad brokers. Had we given one of the brokers we were working with an exclusive representation agreement, we may have lost the best property in town.

Networking Works

The best strategy to find good brokers is to network with other brokers within your geographic area and with community leaders. Having a strong network database to refer to on a regular basis will lead to more real estate opportunities.

As you build your own network database, keep some guidelines in mind:

> ➢ Don't wait to start building your network database until you need someone. Building your network database should be one of your first priorities. Too many people wait to begin until a need arises. They then scramble to find just the right people who can help them. Start building your own list of contacts today so you're not caught off guard.

➢ Always get references from others. Just because someone says they're the "best so-and-so in the business," never take their word for it. After all, do you really think anyone would boast a poor track record? Since you only want to associate with the industry leaders, ask for several references from each person, and then actually check them. Learn if this person is someone you really want to work with in the future. Make sure the person has a reputation for being reliable, fair, and ethical. Those are the kind of people you want to align yourself with.

➢ Attend Chamber of Commerce meetings and exchange business cards. If you want to meet the best people, you have to hang out and mingle where they are. Go to every meeting with a fresh stack of business cards, and hand them out to whomever you'd like to work with in the future. Ask for the other person's card in return. When you get back to your office or to your home, call the people you met to discuss your networking idea further and to learn more about the other person.

➢ Attend other local club meetings. Look in your local newspaper for listings of meetings and functions. Attend those that are of interest, following the same guidelines as for the Chamber of Commerce meetings.

➢ Bring up the topic of networking during business conversations. Whenever you are at a business luncheon or a meeting, always ask others about engineers, architects, attorneys, or real estate brokers whom they have worked with successfully. Exchange business cards with these business associates and write down their suggested contacts on the back of the cards.

➢ Organize your network database into these categories: Architects, Engineers, Investors, Bankers, Mortgage Brokers, Real Estate Brokers, Attorneys, Property Owners, and Contractors.

➢ Develop a Customer Satisfaction Rating Scale based on the recommendations and referrals you receive. Keep the people who get the highest scores as your top three to five professionals in each category.

➤ Contact each of your top five professionals at least monthly. Initially, you may simply want to drop the person a note to introduce yourself. Next, you could call the person and offer to meet for lunch. Then, once you develop some rapport, you could possibly meet for a golf game, tennis match, or some other activity you both enjoy.

➤ Visit your local electronics store and purchase a database program to store and manage your network database. Microsoft® Access™ or Outlook™ (the latter comes with the Microsoft Office® program) are very good spreadsheet programs to manage your database.

When you first start attending the "networking meetings," the Chamber of Commerce meetings, and the other local meetings, you may initially feel very uncomfortable. Don't worry. That is completely normal. The more often you go, the less often you'll have to force a smile as you say "hi" to people you don't know. Soon the networking will become second nature, and you may actually enjoy it. You may even make a friend or two.

Like many people, I used to hate attending networking meetings. The turning point that shifted my displeasure to pleasure occurred while I was aboard an airplane en-route to Ft. Lauderdale. The young woman sitting next to me turned to me and said, "I think we've met before." The conversation proceeded from there. As it turned out, we had met at one of the networking meetings. She worked as an attorney for a law firm, and it just so happened that she was working on a real estate transaction. She told me about it, and we shared ideas. The next real estate project I worked on came from her. Later in my career, her firm represented me on many real estate transactions. It just goes to prove that you never know whom you will meet and how that person may be able to help you in the future.

Because network building is different for each person, you have to develop the procedure that works best for you. Some people thrive in face-to-face encounters; others prefer the telephone; and still others can write a letter so compelling that no one can say "no." Whatever method you choose to contact people, the network database you develop and how you manage it will play a huge role in your future success.

What About Becoming Your Own Broker?

If you wish to limit the number of outside brokers you work with, you can always become your own broker, thereby completely eliminating the need to have a broker assist with your side of the transaction. While you can still enjoy great success without being a broker, many people elect to pursue this route for various reasons.

> ➤ You open yourself up to the vast knowledge of information about properties in your geographic area, which is more readily available to brokerage organizations.

> ➤ You gain a vast amount of knowledge in the preparation of real estate contracts, the closing of contracts, the assessment of real estate tax, and the fundamentals of real estate. This information will be vital as you proceed through your real estate adventure.

> ➤ You accelerate the building of your network database as you share ideas and information with people of similar interests.

> ➤ As you purchase your own properties, you can obtain half of the real estate commission on any property currently listed with other brokers. For properties that are not listed with a broker, you can also collect real estate brokerage commissions. In some cases, you can collect as much as ten percent of the purchase price. That can give you a ten percent down payment.

Immediate income potential is the most important reason for becoming a real estate broker. For most people, obtaining a real estate license and then becoming a broker is the quickest way for them to make money working in a field that allows them to pursue their dream of wealth building. As your career progresses, you'll uncover more personal reasons for pursuing this field, and you'll gain more insider information on ways to successfully work with other real estate brokers.

How To Become Your Own Broker

In order to become a real estate broker, you must pass a state-licensing test. Some states have reciprocal agreements for real estate brokers, which means if you are licensed in one state, you may also be licensed in another state that reciprocates. Be sure to check all licensing laws for each state before you get started.

In Florida, for example, you must complete a license course that varies in length depending upon how much time you are willing to allocate to the course. The most aggressive course is a two-week course. Classes that last longer are usually more beneficial, as they enable people to retain the information better.

Then you must pass the state licensing exam with a grade of 75% or better. That alone will reward you with a salesperson license. To get your broker's license, you must work as an "apprentice" for a full twelve months under an already established broker. At that point there is another set of schooling and testing requirements. Because the requirements constantly change, be sure to obtain the correct information from your appropriate state licensing board.

Once you become licensed as either a salesperson or a broker, you will have to meet continuing education requirements (typically, an exam once every two years). This consists of classroom training where you can update your knowledge on the latest rules and regulations. You will also have to pass a state test to keep your license renewed. While this initial process may sound intimidating, the rewards are far greater than the difficulties. **You can do this.**

The following points show the Florida state licensing requirements. While each state has different specific requirements, they all have some underlying guidelines, which you can glean from this list.

To obtain a Florida real estate license, you must:

> ➤ Successfully complete the Commission approved pre-license course for salespersons (Course 1) consisting of 63 classroom hours of examination.

> ➤ Pass the state licensing salesperson's examination with a grade of at least 75 percent.

To maintain a Florida real estate license, you must:

> ➢ Successfully complete the Commission approved post-licensing course for salespersons consisting of at least 45 classroom hours inclusive of examination prior to the expiration of the initial salesperson's license.

> ➢ Pass the state post-licensing salesperson's examination with a grade of at least 75 percent.

To obtain a Florida real estate broker's license, you must:

> ➢ Have held a current valid real estate salesperson license and complete 12 consecutive months real estate experience during the five year period preceding becoming licensed as a broker.

> ➢ Successfully complete the Commission approved pre-licensing course for brokers (Course 2) consisting of 72 classroom hours inclusive of examination.

> ➢ Pass the state licensing broker examination with a grade of at least 75 percent.

To maintain a Florida real estate broker's license, you must:

> ➢ Successfully complete the Commission approved post-licensing course for brokers consisting on at least 80 classroom hours inclusive of examination prior to the expiration of the initial broker's license.

> ➢ Pass the state post-licensing broker examination with a grade of at least 75 percent.

Important Note: Check with your state's Board of Realtors to learn your exact requirements.

Think Like an Investor

There are many great real estate brokers in this country. Many are excellent salespeople and exceptional at presenting information regarding their listings and those of other associates. Some of these great brokers are very content where they are professionally and do not want to take the risk of investing or owning their own properties.

Other great brokers actively seek out information on how to get to the ownership level so they can build some real wealth of their own. These people are very successful with their brokerage businesses and make a very good living. Although their knowledge of the real estate business, along with their negotiating skills, is tremendous, what holds them back from succeeding at ownership is that they think like a broker and not like an investor/owner.

In their defense, changing your thinking is easier said than done. For example, have you ever tried to learn a new skill? It may have been inline skating, golf, or a musical instrument. Do you remember how hard it was at first? However, most likely, after you practiced, it gradually became easier. That's why as you change your thinking from that of being a broker to that of being an investor/owner, it's important to do so in small, consistent steps.

Here's how: If you are a broker reading this book and you want to become the investor/owner, start by committing right now to investing some amount of your savings into the next real estate project you want to sell or buy. If you are just beginning in the real estate business, you can start by committing to completing this book and all the exercises within. These are just some ideas on how you can start right now and take that first small step towards success.

So, what exactly is the difference in thinking between a broker and an investor/owner? Below is a partial listing of some of the qualities that make for great owners and great brokers. Note the significant differences. This illustrates how sales and wealth building are two very different practices.

Some Qualities of Great	
Owners	**Brokers**
Keen sense of risk management	Modest concern for risk management
Job accelerates at closing	Job ends at closing
Long-term thinker	Short-term thinker
Personal money at risk	No personal money at risk
Objective thinker	Subjective thinker
Investment return oriented	Sales commission oriented

mastering all the techniques presented in this book is essential for you to chase and catch the deal of a lifetime. Whichever route you choose, give your decision 100% effort and consistent daily action. Anything less will always leave you wondering "what if?" By giving 100%, you will know your true capabilities. After all, you are striving for new results in your life, and you are certainly worth 100%.

> The direction you choose is yours for the taking.

Chapter Two:

Anchoring Ideas ~ An Exercise

Shop
for New
Success Ideas

Whether or not you think obtaining your real estate license is for you, do this exercise. It will reveal to you valuable information regarding the real estate business and your own future objectives. As stated previously, obtaining your real estate license is not mandatory for you to successfully complete this program; however, mastery of the techniques and strategies shared in this book is essential to your future success.

Devote time this week to learning the real estate licensing requirements for your state. Review the qualifications and decide for yourself whether this option is for you. Invest at least an additional week to think it through. By doing this research you may also identify a real estate course that interests you independent of any licensing course requirements. Check with your local Board of Realtors for courses and schedules.

Chapter Three ~

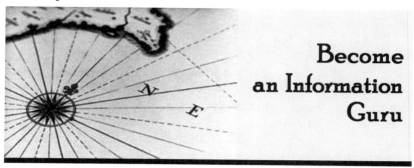

Become an Information Guru

Befor you go out and look for a piece of property to invest in, you need to first understand the big picture. Once you have a firm grasp of the fundamental principles, then you can fine-tune your vision and find a specific property. This simple approach continually nets far greater results than anyone can ever imagine.

With that in mind, the first thing you'll need is a map. If you don't own one, be sure to buy one right away. Also, investing in a software-mapping program is extremely helpful. Today's software programs are very effective and highly detailed. They provide a significant amount of real estate and general vicinity information, such as points of interest, places of business, government offices, etc.

If you don't want to buy a software-mapping program and prefer to work solely on a paper map, that's okay. Just realize that you'll have to work five times harder than someone who does invest in technology. This is not to say that it can't be done. Before computers became so prevalent and helpful, those in real estate had no choice but to map properties the old-fashioned way. As long as you're committed to making this work and you stay focused, you will succeed.

For those who do want to work less and earn more, check out the Microsoft® mapping software called Streets and Trips™. It's one of the best mapping programs available, and you can find it at most electronics stores that sell software.

As soon as you get your software, install it and become familiar with how it works. This is the start required to build a strong foundation that will support you for a lifetime of victories. While learning a new computer program may be hard, remember that the more you practice, the easier it gets.

With the new software, your goal is to uncover the ultimate treasure and find the ideal site. So let's find it.

"X" Marks the Spot

First, open your map or mapping program. Next, select your desired geographic area, preferably within ten miles of your home. Pick one municipality – one governing body – again, preferably in the town, city, or county in which you live. For now, work just in this focused geographic area. You can expand your territory as you gain more knowledge and learn how to apply it.

Study everything about your selected geographic area. Where are the business sectors, the schools, the retail merchants, the government offices, and the residential areas? Familiarize yourself with the road system. Are there highways and expressways? Are there dirt roads? Where are the traffic lights or traffic circles? How are the roads built? Are they positioned logically in a grid format, or are they old-fashioned winding roads with no apparent order? You want to know as much about the territory as possible.

Whether you are using a mapping software program or mapping by hand on a paper map, be sure you thoroughly know what each symbol or color code means. You want to get to the point where you can glance at the map, see the various colors and symbols, and instantly know what everything means and where it is. When you're building your wealth, there's no time for guessing. You want the answers planted firmly in your mind so you don't have to waste time looking up key codes.

Should you ask others how they use and read their maps? Sure. But realize that what works for one person may not work for another. Get some ideas from others, but in the end, your mapping system has to work for you and only you. So investigate various mapping programs and find the one that you're most comfortable with. This step is important, because it's the key to the treasure. As long as you can read your map quickly and easily, you can find the goldmine property.

Five Steps to Becoming an Information Guru

Your level of success in this field will depend on the amount of information you can amass regarding your geographic area and the properties contained within. While learning everything there is to know about a city, town, or county may seem intimidating, it's really quite simple...providing that you follow certain steps.

1. **Get in the car and drive every street, every dirt road, and every path to gain knowledge of your area.**
    Notice what is happening, such as new subdivisions being developed or new roads being constructed. In fact, any new construction is noteworthy. Keep a logbook or a mini tape recorder in your car so you can take notes as you drive. After your drive, transfer all the information you gathered to your main map. Keep this map as your working tool, completely updated with the latest information on it. In order to keep your map current, you must consistently drive your territory.

    (Hint: Schedule the time for these drives. They're that important. Work them into your daily routine. For example, take a new route to and from work each day. It will save you time. You may even stumble upon a great find.)

2. **Schedule time to visit your local building and planning department to dig up any new real estate news.**
    In that office you can find new roads, new subdivisions, and anything else under development. The information you obtain here will be valuable for your adventure. Most of the information is in the public domain. Therefore, it's free. The only things you would have to pay for are photocopies, maps, and any other supplies.

3. **Become well versed in the zoning laws and land use changes in your community.**
    While this information is also public knowledge, it will take you a bit longer to obtain it, so patience is necessary. As you work with zoning authorities, remember that a pleasant personality always helps. If you become frustrated with the people from whom you are seeking help, you will get nowhere.
    Why is working with the zoning board so important? Well, you might uncover a properly zoned property that is underutilized. You can then purchase it and place a new use on it that will pay higher rents, significantly increasing the property's value. I recall one instance where I stumbled across a multi-family zoned parcel located in an area that was thought to be exhausted of any further multi-family zoning. The belief was that only single-family zoning was remaining in the area. The value of that find alone was huge.

4. **Visit the local property appraiser's office.**
   Learn how to look up the ownership of a particular property.
   The personnel there will be glad to help you, as long as you
   remain polite and respectful. They can also show you an aerial
   view of your territory, and instruct you on how to look up
   foreclosures that are pending as well as new sales, which will
   give you an idea of comparable selling prices in your territory.
   While you can check online for this information, a personal
   visit to the property appraiser's office will reap more benefits
   than the impersonal online information. You can obtain answers
   to your questions much easier with an in person visit.

5. **Read the real estate section of your local**
   Sunday newspaper.
   Here you will find valuable information regarding your
   territory, including properties for sale, sale prices, and new
   developments.

Face the Facts

The better you get at collecting data, the more of it you will have. The
trick now becomes organizing the information in a way that makes
sense...and that makes your job easier. Many people who are new to
real estate find themselves initially overwhelmed with lots of information. If this happens to you, rest assured that it is normal. In their quest
to gather all the data they can, new real estate professionals routinely
find themselves with notes upon notes scattered throughout their office
and car.

I call this being in "ferret" mode. It's when you continually gather
information, and then often re-gather the same information because you
were disorganized and misplaced the information the first time you obtained it. The solution? Spend time the same day you obtain the information organizing it; otherwise, you will misplace it, forget its importance, or even forget its meaning.

Your goal should be to become a "beaver." Why a beaver? Beavers
are great dam builders. When they gather a piece of wood for the dam,
they immediately put it into its place. So when it comes to organizing
your information, do it immediately. If you make it a habit to always
carry a map and notebook with you, you can immediately place your
detailed information on the map (your wood on the dam). This one step
will save you a tremendous amount of time; and in this business, time is
money.

Once you transfer all your data onto your map, you should start to notice areas of interest – places where there is lots of sales activity or construction, or anything else that would increase a location's value. Consistency of information will help you determine fact from fiction. As you start to see these areas of interest, make a special note or circle the area with a written note beside the circle.

Figure 3a below shows an example of this process. It represents a portion of a national study I conducted during a site selection for a major national corporation. I traveled the East Coast of the United States and searched for 25 sites. Notice the actual site selections in comparison to the data around it. You can use this study to develop your own site selection process for all types of real estate. As you begin the process yourself, you may find it easier to print the map and pencil in all your data as you find it. It's much easier to take the paper map with you than to lug your entire computer with you.

By giving yourself the overall macro picture of the area, the property with the best location will jump out at you. Developing this complete overview is the only way you should ever purchase property, whether it is a single-family home, an apartment complex, or a commercial property. This is a critical first step in any real estate purchase. Allow time for preparation and you will see huge profits.

Figure 3a - Mapping Your Vicinity:

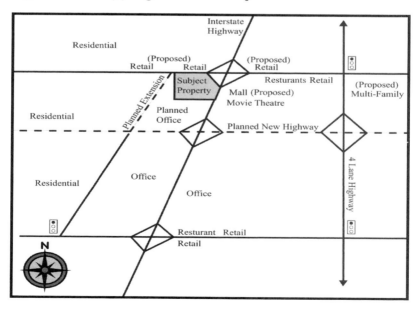

No Ceiling Earnings

You now have a foundation started for your new way of working and building wealth. If you're like most people, you may be used to a job where you work eight hours a day and receive a weekly paycheck. This process will slowly transform your thinking on the best way to earn money and the whole concept of "job security."

Once you get started in real estate full time, you will not have a guaranteed salary. However, you will also not have any cap on your earning potential. This makes your income possibilities limitless. The secret is to work smart. You must realize that time is money, and anything you can do to save time will equate to more money in your pocket.

Practice good habits, utilize available technology, and invest in a good mapping software program.

The rewards are fabulous.

Chapter Three:
Anchoring Ideas ~ An Exercise

Scout
Your
Territory

Gather your territory information. Remember, you are not looking for anything specific. **This is the BIG picture view of your territory**. Refer to the chapter for your process. In a nut shell:

> ➢ Drive your territory and write or record your notes. Transfer all important findings onto your map.

> ➢ Visit your local planning and building department. Transfer all important findings onto your map.

> ➢ Review zoning laws and land use laws in your territory. Transfer all important findings onto your map.

> ➢ Visit your local property appraiser's office. Transfer all important findings onto your map.

> ➢ Read the real estate section of your local newspaper's Sunday edition. Transfer all important findings onto your map.

> ➢ Introduce yourself to two real estate brokers who have a lot of "For Sale" signs posted in your territory. Ask them general questions so you can get a feel for the area. What new projects are planned? Where are the best areas for investment, in their opinion? Let them know that you are in the early stages of researching the area for potential investments. Encourage them to send you information as they see fit. Transfer all important findings onto your map.

> ➢ Keep all the information in a folder in written form.

Chapter Four ~

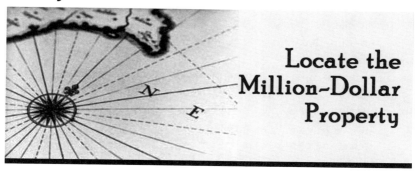

Locate the Million-Dollar Property

Y ou've certainly heard the old phrase: "The three most important things to consider when buying real estate are location, location, location." Is that phrase true? Well…yes…and no.

Most experienced and successful investors cringe when they hear someone utter those three "L" words together. While it's good to hear that the general population has some idea of real estate principles, more often than not the person touting the "location" phrase has just enough knowledge to be dangerous. It's similar to all those Monday morning quarterbacks. Criticizing something – whether it's a football game or a real estate purchase – is always easier after the fact.

The truth is that not many people, seasoned real estate people included, really understand what makes a poor location, what makes a good location, and what makes a great location. For you, though, that's about to change.

The previous chapters were the building blocks to get you to this point. Gathering the information, organizing the information while managing your time, and understanding that time is money are all important factors. Now you will learn how to take those skills a step further. By building on your core knowledge with some location principles, you will be able to distinguish the difference between a true property gem and a fancily-packaged dud.

Beware of the Watch Salesman in the Trench Coat

The first important principle to remember is that the property's selling price, terms, and condition are irrelevant right now. You are only interested in finding that gem of a property. This strategy alone will launch your profits.

Too many people begin their property search looking for a "deal." Unfortunately, some sellers play into that mentality, advertising their properties with words like "below market pricing," "great terms," "a steal," and "won't last long at this price." These are all great attention getters, but if the property is so great, why does the seller need to use such terminology at all?

Sellers who position their properties with sensational descriptives are like the watch salesmen in trench coats who "hawk" fakes of expensive brand name watches and represent them as authentic. The bottom line is that if the property needs that kind of price promoting to get people to pay attention to it, then it's probably not the great location you desire. Gather the facts before letting the excitement of the moment overtake you.

At this point many people usually ask, *"But what if the property owner is having financial troubles and the economy is in bad shape and the seller really needs to sell? Wouldn't the property be marketed as 'price reduced' to move it?"*

Even in this scenario, the same answer holds true. Location is the key to your profits. If the property has a great location and the circumstances are such that financial troubles and poor economic conditions add to the seller's woes, then in the real world this property would never even make it to the market. In fact, chances are that the property would sell before the news hit the street. With a high-quality location, there's a good chance that an attorney would be working with the owner. This same legal counsel may even know of an investor or an investor group that would be willing to step in and help before the property even got to the broker or to the market for sale. **It's called networking.**

The lesson: If your location is less than first-rate, you can expect the outcome of the project to suffer a less than favorable fate. Do not price shop property, and beware of the superficial deal.

A Picture is Worth a Million Dollars

The following are two maps. Figure 4a shows an example of a property with a good location; the buyer increased the property's value by maximizing its use.

(Hint: The right user will make your profits increase, as you'll soon learn.)

Figure 4a ~ Example of a Good Resturant Location:

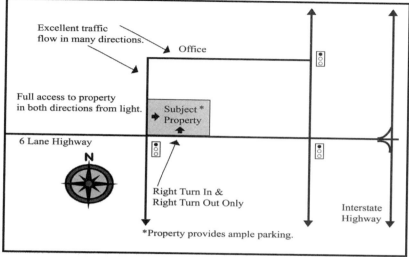

1. Property has full access from the main roadway at the traffic signal.
2. Surrounding offices are excellent for lunchtime business.
3. Easy access to roadway in all directions. Interstate Highway can draw from larger area.

Figure 4b - Example of a Poor Resturant Location:

Figure 4b shows what a poor location looks like. The broker for this particular site is marketing the property for a restaurant. Can you determine why the property is a poor location?

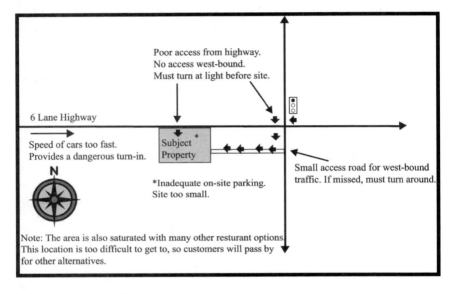

1. Speed zone is 45 mph, making the vehicle speed too fast.
2. In one direction there is no braking time until after the vehicle passes the site.
3. Property is too small, making parking inadaquate.
4. There are too many other resturant choices in the area with easier access.

Become a Road Warrior

The second important principle to remember is that driving your territory on a regular basis will make you a master at picking the finest real estate site. For many real estate investors, their car is their mobile office. All they need is a cell phone and their files, and they're set to work from the road. An administrative assistant can easily keep the non-mobile office running smoothly.

This is an important step, because if you are not driving your territory looking at properties, and reviewing areas, then you are going to be out of business in a hurry. What should you be looking for as you drive? Glad you asked…

With every piece of property you look at, you must always remember that the end user of the property determines its ultimate value. Now here's the catch: Each end user (the person who will be operating, living, and "using" this property) views the property differently. So, your job is to become an expert in your market as well as an expert in the needs of each business so that the ideal end user for the location immediately jumps out at you. That way there's no second guessing as to whom or what the property is best suited for. For example, a one-acre commercial corner at the major intersection of your city or town is obviously not an ideal residential site. However, it could be a great location for a fast food store or convenience store/gas station. Of course, you need much more additional information to determine the precise end user, but knowing your territory will help you instantly narrow down your market for each location.

What to Look For

As you examine each location, analyze the property for its practicality.
Some points to consider include:

> ## Proximity to Shopping Centers

Is the property close to shopping centers for the convenience of
its users? For example, it might be effective to locate a small
clothing store or a gas station next to a large shopping mall.
Why? Because thousands of people are coming to the mall on a
daily basis. Everyone loves convenience. If people can get everything they need near the mall, it will save them a lot of time.

**(Hint: That million-dollar treasure might be hiding in close
proximity to a regional mall.)**

> ## Proximity to Schools

Examine the local school systems, determining which are the
"best" and "worst" schools. There are schools that have better
reputations within the community than others, and you can discover the reputations by meeting with other real estate brokers.
You can also look up school statistics to back up what brokers
are saying by contacting the Board of Education for the local
area.

**(Hint: You might find that property values in certain school
districts are higher than other school districts. Properties
may also sell faster in certain school districts than in
others.)**

Don't forget about colleges and universities; they are schools
too. The huge student population will require services and goods,
much like any small town or community. Locating a business
or service industry near a university or college may reap great
rewards.

➢ ## Look at Transportation Routes to & from Work

Are the roads easily accessible, as interstate highways typically are, or are they small and congested? Transportation routes do make a difference. Put yourself in the customer's shoes and ask, *"Is this traffic and the frequent delays worth my time spent traveling to this location?"* If not, determine if there is a better roadway that is more convenient. Know the customers and their driving habits.

➢ ## Look at Proximity to Churches & Recreation Areas

Recreation areas include parks, golf courses, lakes, rivers, beaches, etc. People enjoy their leisure time and they love convenience, so you should note the locations and types of recreation available nearby. If the property is located near a body of water, you must know where the water flows to and from. Having water on the property is usually good, but consider the fact that many locations can be enhanced with a water view. In addition, find out if the water flows to a larger body of water that will allow for boating or other recreation. Is it a good fishing lake? As you ask these questions, keep the potential end user in mind, because this may make a difference in the value of the property. For example, a potential restaurant owner may like the view of the water from the building's dining room. If all other characteristics, such as zoning, meet the buyer's criteria, you could potentially receive more value for the property than a small apartment complex owner might pay. **Again, know the customer.**

➢ ## Determine Whether the Area is in an Upswing or Downswing

You can obtain this information by meeting with other realtors or brokers. If the area is in an upswing, your appreciation in value will be greater and will come more quickly than a property that is in a down cycle. Also consider the fact that different types of properties move in cycles. For example, at times you will notice more of a demand for apartment complexes than say office buildings or land. Financial markets have a lot to do with these cycles, as do the economics of supply and demand. When there are more apartments than renters, then the demand for apartment complexes decreases and the value of the complexes follows. The opposite is also true. When there are more renters than apartments to rent, demand and value increase. The same holds true for other commercial properties. Talking to lenders can also help you gauge what's moving. If you determine that an area is in an upswing, realize that now is the time to buy. While you shouldn't try to perfectly time the deals, you should always include timing in your considerations as you master the complete program.

➢ ## Look at Traffic Patterns

How easy is it to get to the property? Can you make a left turn onto the property, heading in the opposite direction? Some properties do not allow for this left turn; in that case, it would not be the preferable property. Is the property on a road curve? On road curves (refer to Figure 4c below), there is always a concave and convex side. The concave side is always the preferred side, because your line of sight is far greater than on the convex side. As you can see in the drawing, people driving on the road will have time to spot the property that is located on the concave side. If "X" is your store, customers will be able to spot your sign and make the appropriate traffic adjustments so they can enter the driveway. On the convex side, the opposite happens, and more than likely the driver will not see the business in time and will speed past the property.

Figure 4c – Example of Lines of Site:

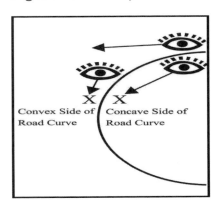

➤   Evaluate Existing Competition

What stores or shops or services are currently in the area? Are they all big mega marts, or are they small mom and pop shops? What specifically is each store or service selling? Is there a predominance of food stores, restaurants, gift shops, gas stations, clothes stores, offices, apartments, etc? Scout the area and know precisely what kinds of properties are nearby and how many of each. Is the location along potential customers' existing travel routes, or will they have to use other routes to get to you? Customers will always use the routes they are accustomed to. How does the location stack up any competition? Does the competing property provide better access? Can you see the competing property better? Do potential customers pass the competition before your potential property? How does your parking compare? If answers to these questions are negative then your competition has "out located" you. Think twice before investing.

➤   Determine Which Corner of the Intersection
       is a Better Property

The near corner, prior to the light, is not the preferable corner for any commercial user, unless it is the only corner remaining. If you have a choice, you should seek out the far corner. The corner past the light on the road with the higher traffic count determines the far corner, as you will notice in Figure 4d below. Traffic does not back up in front of the far corner property, which makes for easy ingress and egress. In the near corner, traffic will back up in front of the site and prevent customer access.

Figure 4d – Comparing Corners:

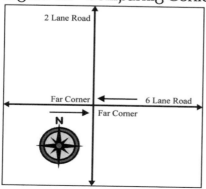

Put the High Payoff Client in the Proper Place

For every piece of property you look at, analyze the following points:

➢ ## Identify Existing Competition

You must identify all existing competition (users with same products or services that compete for the same customers) when selecting a commercial site. In addition, identify existing same entity users for cannibalization (when the same entity "eats" its own customers because its locations are too close given the demographics of the market). Both cases test whether the market is deep enough (big enough) to handle the additional store. If the market is not deep enough, then there are not enough customers in that market for that user's specific products or services

➢ ## Look For Holes

What's missing for the commercial mix? Are there lots of places to eat dinner, but no breakfast spots? Do people have to travel far just to get to a pharmacy? Is there only one gas station servicing the whole area? What services or goods would you need or want if you lived or worked in the area?

➢ ## Study The Demographics

What do the demographics tell you about the area and the people's needs? What's the predominant age of the people in the area? What's the median income level? Where do these people work? Are the majority of jobs available white collar or blue collar? Industrial or technical? What are people's spending habits? Intimately know the demographics of your territory. National Decision Systems is a company that provides such demographic services. You can hire them for your specific property. The costs vary depending upon the work you are requiring.

> ## Parcel Size, Zoning, Cost & Permits

Is the lot too big? Too small? Is parking an issue? Is there easy access to the site? What has the county zoning board deemed the property acceptable for? Would that zoning decision support the ideal end user's objectives? What does the property cost? Understand that "property cost" is a function of the occupancy cost or rent an end user may pay for the use of the property and the profit for the investor. In working this formula backwards, the rent or usage fee an end user can pay for a property is directly conditioned upon the demographics of the area. In addition, the demographics of the area will determine what profit potential exists for the end user. This holds true for any kind of property.

For example, an office user, such as an attorney or a CPA, can only charge a certain dollar amount for his or her services based upon the demographics of the area. This limits the amount of rent he or she would be willing to pay, as it relates to the profit the end user is willing to accept. In retail, the relationship is the same. Apartments hold a similar relationship. The ideal question to ask yourself when evaluating a property in this manner is: *"What would the end users be willing to pay given the demographics of the neighborhood and the profit potential they can generate from locating there?"* Is the site cost-efficient for your end users compared to sales projections? Finally, can you get the property permitted for what your end user would want?

Figure 4e – Site One Map:
Ideal for a gas station, why?

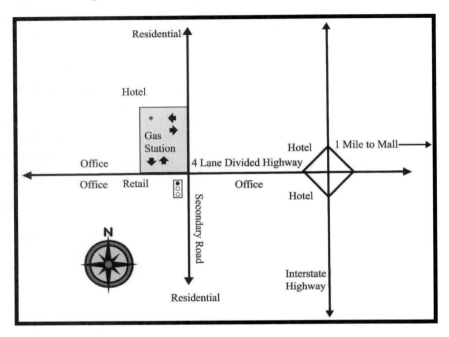

1. Far corner to the intersection.
2. Right turn in / Right turn out only on four-lane divided highway, but full access on secondary road.
3. Site is large enough.
4. Elevation of site rises at * and zoning will allow signage to be seen from highway.
5. Surrounding area has large base demographics to support sales.
6. Traffic counts on main road are above 27,000 vehicles per day (V.P.D.)
7. Secondary road leads back into residential areas.

Figure 4f - Site Two Map:
Ideal for an in-line retail store, why?

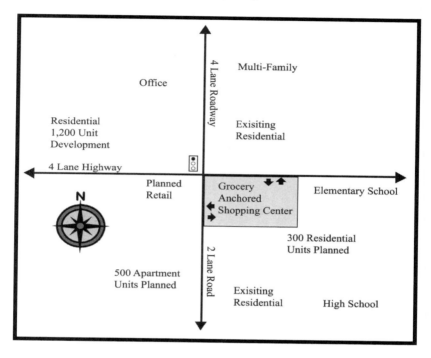

1. Far corner to the intersection.
2. Full access to both roads and the light.
3. Site is large enough, making parking adequate.
4. The demographic base is good. Plus future growth is good with several planned developments.
5. Traffic counts on main road and secondary roads are growing.

Figure 48 – Site Three Map:
Ideal for residential, why?

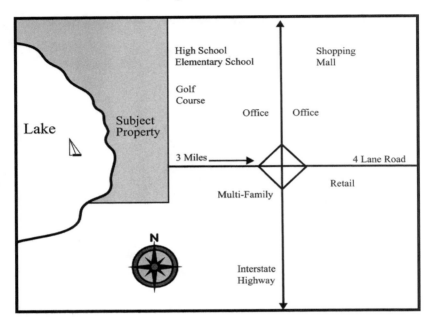

1. Lake front property with unobstructed view.
2. Access to recreational amenities and services such as golf, shopping, lake, and schools.
3. Easy access to major interstate and other roadways.

Figure 4h – Site Four Map: Ideal for office, why?

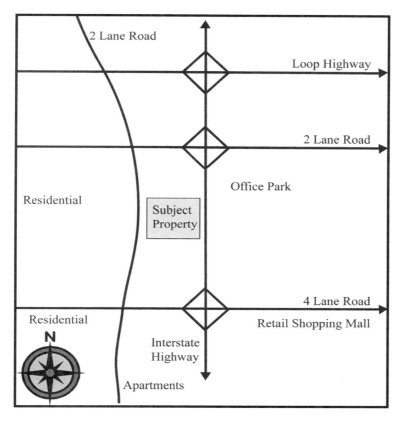

1. Excellent access and visibility from highway.
2. Many access points to subject property, thereby eliminating potential traffic congestion.
3. Existing office park is 100% leased with escalating rents and high demand.
4. Great employment pool based upon demographic studies.
5. Growth area.

Real Life Payoff Profiles

While all these principles and steps may seem like a lot to master, they really do come together quite naturally as you are locating properties. Let me share with you some examples from my own career to illustrate how certain principles effortlessly work off each other.

Example One – Cannibals in the Midst

A broker once presented me with a vacant twenty-acre parcel of land for my consideration to develop. The broker, who I regard as one of the better brokers in the country, felt that the property was ideal for a national supermarket chain. I wasn't so sure, so I did some homework.

In the analysis, my associates and I identified all the grocery-anchored competition within a three to five-mile area, and we identified existing stores of that supermarket chain in the same area. We then identified the different traffic patterns, showing where customers might be traveling from in order to get to the other grocery stores. We also requested that the supermarket firm conduct an operations analysis of its existing stores to determine whether cannibalization would occur if they were to open a new store at this site.

The grocery operator discovered that there would be a significant amount of cannibalization. In some cases, that would be fine, provided the company was going to capture more of the market from competitors by opening a new store. But, in this case, the market did not have the depth to support an additional grocery store in the area.

The real estate departments of many retailers, particularly grocery chains, have extensive data as to where their shoppers are coming from, based on zip code and street address. Therefore, they can make a fairly quick analysis of customer traffic patterns and the amount of cannibalization that would take place.

(Note: For grocery stores, people tend to travel a maximum of three miles to get their groceries. Soft goods retailers, such as apparel stores, tend to draw customers from a five to ten-mile radius. Malls tend to draw from a much larger radius, usually exceeding ten miles.)

An old adage in the real estate business is that no retailer likes to be the one to break new ground. An exception to this is a grocery-anchored shopping center. As long as the demographics are there, and the new location meets the chain's expansion and supply plans, the chain will break that pattern and make a pioneering move in order to capture more market share.

Example Two - The Road to Riches

In one instance, a fellow investor used his knowledge of zoning laws to his benefit. He heard through the grapevine that the county planned to extend a major roadway. After doing some checking, he confirmed the information. He also learned that the planned roadway extension was going to connect into a major existing roadway, creating a huge four-lane, traffic-signalized intersection.

Further analysis revealed that the new road extension would connect a major part of the city, cutting travel times in half. This would generate additional traffic on the new road. For days, he drove the area where the newly created intersection would be. He called on every "For Sale" sign in the area and put together his overview map.

Finally, the property ripe for his investment jumped out at him. He discovered that a nicely located property close to the proposed new intersection was under-zoned. Based on the facts he had gathered, this property could be re-zoned from its current agricultural zoning to one for heavier commercial uses. He also checked with an engineer and learned that the property could be re-zoned now; he wouldn't have to wait for the new road to be completed. Hence, he would immediately create a much more valuable piece of property.

He had now identified a location with great potential that was already priced right. The key was to move quickly before someone else uncovered the same treasure. He immediately purchased the property for its asking price.

He tore down the existing house on the property, and within one year, when the news of the new extension road hit the streets and construction had started, the property instantly doubled in value. He could have sold then and seen a handsome profit. However, he now has plans for a development, which he will lease to potential tenants. This option allows him to sell later and earn roughly four times his original investment. Otherwise, he can hold the property for many years and, depending on his ownership structure and financing arrangement, enjoy a huge cash flow from the property through rental income. By taking his time with the upfront research, he created long-term opportunities for himself.

You Can Do the Same Thing!

Example Three ~ A 300% Return

A few years ago, our partnership purchased a nice corner of commercial property with an exsiting gas station on it. The Department of Public Works had plans to double the size of the road that ran by the property. If the state was willing to spend millions of dollars to widen the road, then we figured that the traffic flow must be increasing rapidly. Increased traffic often translates into increased value in commercial property.

In this example, our homework paid off. The value of our property did increase with the increase in traffic. In addition, the State Department of Public Works paid us fair market value for the section of our property they needed to widen the road.

(Hint: Whenever the state wants to buy land from you, get yourself a good attorney versed in state condemnation proceedings.)

The road widening shaved off a good portion of our property, making it now too small for the gas station. However, the sale of land to the state yielded us $150,000, so we repositioned the property and built a small retail complex on it, thus pushing the property's value up. Our market studies prior to purchase limited our risk and helped us turn what appeared to be a less than favorable circumstance into a cash return of about 300%.

Example Four ~ Fishing for "The Big One"

Years ago when I was just learning the business, I had the opportunity to meet many interesting people and large real estate owners. One particular owner was an older man. At the time, I was twenty-one years old, and he was a southern gentleman in his mid sixties. He took me freshwater bass fishing one day to teach me the greatest lesson in real estate location.

"You need a fishing lesson, so we're going fishing," he said in his southern drawl.

"I don't have time to go fishing. I have work to do," I said impatiently.

He countered, "Look, son, (he called me son when he was frustrated with me, even though he wasn't my father) this here fishing trip will be the best lesson you could ever learn about real estate location. Now let's go!"

Reluctantly, I went.

I still pull lessons from that single fishing trip to this day. But the secret about real estate location revealed during that trip is what I want to share with you now.

As we boarded the small boat, he said to me, "We got to go where the fish live or where the fish 'hang out.' Now I know where those spots are because I have driven this lake for forty years. I have studied every lily pad on this pond. I know the patterns of the fish. We might not be able to see them, but I know they are there. They have been swimming this same pattern for years. All we have to do is wiggle that little rubber worm past them enough times, until they can't stand it, and then they will take the bait. You follow me?"

"No," I replied, "but I am sure I'll get it three weeks from now."

"Youth is wasted on the young," he muttered.

I have never caught more fish in a single day than I did that day. And, that night, the real lesson hit me:

Everything I Needed To Know About High-Quality Locations I Learned Bass Fishing

➤ Hang out where the fish live – Know your territory

➤ Look under every lily pad – Know every property that is for sale and not for sale

➤ Watch where the fish swim – Know customer travel patterns

➤ Identify the lake's water flow – Know transportation routes

➤ Watch how the fish swim – Know habits

➤ Identify which fish swim together and the "schools" – Know neighborhoods

➤ Learn which section of the lake attracts the most fish – Know recreation areas and fun spots

➤ Watch where the number of fish fluctuates – Know whether the area is in an upswing or downswing

➤   Find out what the fish do during the day – Know where people work

➤   Know the number of both big fish and little fish – Know your demographics

➤   Determine what will make the fish bite – Know what customers spend their money on

➤   Determine what to bait your hook with – Know what customers like to eat and do for fun

When you put these factors together, you can catch "the big one."

And that, my friends, is

No Fish Story!

Anchoring Ideas ~ An Exercise

Become the
Location
Master

Take as much time as you need to complete the following exercise.

> ➢ Drive your highlighted area of interest, noting anything special that strikes you.

> ➢ Note all properties for sale in your highlighted area.

> ➢ Visit the local planning and building department and dig up any new and specific information regarding your highlighted area.

> ➢ Contact all properties for sale in your highlighted area and fill out a property information sheet for each (on the next page see Figure 4i Site Data Sheet).

Figure 4i ~ Site Data Sheet

SITE DATA SHEET

Project: _____

Property Location: _____

_____

Contact Information

_____

_____

_____

Statistics

1. Parcel Size: _____ Zoning: _____   Asking Price: _____

2. Building Size: _____

3. Tenant Mix/Rents: _____

4. Critical Dates: _____
   a) Purchase Contract: _____
      Effective Date: _____
      Expiration Date for Due Diligence: _____
      Expiration Date for Building Permit: _____
      Closing Date: _____
      Other Key Dates:_____

   b) Lease with: _____

   c) Lease with: _____

   d) Lease with: _____

   e) ETC   _____

5. Development Loan: _____
      Term: _____
      Interest Rate: _____
      Financing Fee: _____
      ETC   _____

6. ETC _____

   _____

Chapter Five ~

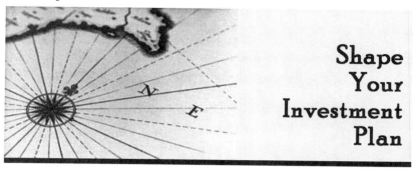

Shape Your Investment Plan

Provided you have done the mapping and the market studies described in the previous chapters, you may have a property that seems interesting and jumps out at you as a potentially great location. Now is when you can construct a preliminary pro forma investment analysis – a form specifying the potential cash flow and investment returns of a particular project. The objective is to think through the investment. Think of it as if you were creating your own crystal ball. This is your chance to look into the future to determine how you would like to see the investment turn out, given the data you currently have available.

It's important to remain completely objective when completing this step. In other words, do not let your emotions or personal opinions influence the analysis. Make sure that any assumptions you make are based only on the facts gathered. If you base the data on your opinions, you will lose.

The three main ingredients of the preliminary plan are:

1. Your location map with all the market details, such as zoning, site size, site dimensions, the property's current asking price, area demographics, new roads, traffic flows, accessibility, potential end user profile (or if the user is already renting the property, the current rental income from the property), taxes, property cost, existing competition, and current rents from existing competition.

2. Your market studies with pricing of other properties in the area. You can obtain this information by contacting the listing agents for competing properties.

3. Your investment summary and funding requirements, which you are about to create now.

Factors to Consider

Your investment analysis will be made up of both tangible and intangible items. Tangible items include everything from the property location to the financing structure, while intangible items include such things as perceived risk, appreciation, and depreciation of the property. Let's look at each in detail.

Tangible Items

➢ **Property Location**

Since no one can change a property's geographic position, most seasoned investors know the importance of a high-quality location. Your job is to define the property's location, show it to be the best for a potential user, and convince your investor of its promise.

➢ **Market Rents & Market Prices**

Obtain comparable pricing on competing properties from other brokers and landlords. This data will provide valuable information in your analysis of the property's financial prospects. You can also visit the property appraiser's office and obtain comparable sales data on properties that have recently sold. Another way to obtain this information is by networking with real estate appraisers. Having a real estate appraiser as a partner in your projects can prove to be very valuable.

➢ **Financing**

From your banking relationships, discussed in earlier chapters, you can obtain financing terms currently available.

➢   **Equity**

Equity is the difference between the total project cost and the available financing. It details how much money you will need to invest in the project.

➢   **Return on Equity (ROE)**

This is the investment return you expect on the required equity. Return on equity represents the quotient obtained when you divide net income from operations by your required equity. The number is usually expressed as a percentage.

Return on Equity Formula:
$$\frac{\text{Net Income}}{\text{Equity}} = \text{ROE}$$

Intangible Items

➢   **Risk Tolerance**

Risk tolerance is different for each person. Creating the optimum balance of risk versus the return on investment is an art that makes real estate enticing to many people. When you can define that optimum balance, you will create a winning property for you and your investors. It is much more art than science.

Risk varies from one investor's interpretation of the facts to another's and depends on the person's individual belief in the reliability of those facts. That's why it is important to gather all the facts prior to making any kind of proposal. Regardless of what the data says, there is an element of the human factor that we cannot remove when calculating risk. Risk is ultimately a thought process that involves careful evaluation.

So, how do you evaluate risk? Is risk a solely personal preference? We could say that Risk equals the Quality of the Facts (Investment Opportunity) compared to the Cash On Cash Return of another perceived safer investment such as CDs, Treasury Bills, etc., minus the Opportunity Loss.

Opportunity Loss equals the perceived value of the investment returns lost by not investing and taking into account inflation, taxes, and other outside factors. For example, a CD at five percent may sound like a safe rate, unless, of course, inflation is running at four percent. In that case, the five percent rate is now only a one percent rate. Likewise, a thirty percent return on a real estate project might be more risky, but you could gain a twenty-six percent return taking into account inflation. If you decide not to invest in the project, your opportunity loss would be twenty-five percent, assuming the quality of the investment facts to be high. That is to say it's a lost opportunity for you to invest your money.

Risk is also a personal preference. Given everyone's individual needs, some investors can tolerate risk more than others, and that's okay. Each individual has to make up his or her own mind regarding risks versus the rewards (returns) he or she sees generated from the risks taken. Here's an example: Two people are deciding whether to bungee jump. Person A and Person B each has a different view of the situation. To determine if the risk is acceptable, they each need to review the hard data.

1. The fall is 100 feet.
2. The bungee cords are all new and have never been used before.
3. The harness is also brand new and has never been used before.
4. The jump is off a bridge.
5. The river below the bridge is ten feet deep.
6. Should the rope break, the landing would most likely kill the person.

Would You Jump?

Person A decides not to jump; Person B is ready to go for it. Even though they both analyzed the same facts, they each had a different perception of the risks involved in the bungee jump versus the benefits he or she would get from the jump. So given the facts, their risk/reward factor is different.

The above is a simple example to assist in the explanation of assessing risk. Very often, people want to know what they can do to significantly lower their risk factor on new projects now, when they don't have years of experience to back them up.

The best advice is to **_get in the TUB._** That is:
1. **Treat** people fairly, honestly, and with respect.
2. **Use** objective analysis. Keep your emotions and opinions in check.
3. **Base** decisions on facts. Do all your research and homework up front. Take your time and do a thorough job. Don't cut corners here. You will need all the knowledge and facts gained in the information gathering stage to make good decisions.

In real estate, analyzing risk becomes more artful as you master the secrets of finding the ideal location, solving problems in early stages of due diligence, negotiating for your own best interests, and only closing a transaction after you have done your homework and have developed a completely clear plan. Mastering these four components and practicing them daily will make you better at assessing your own risk and minimizing risk in each of your transactions.

Remember that there is an element of risk in every business plan, so don't get discouraged should a particular investor reject your proposal. Instead, listen to what the investor has to say and question why. Once you understand the other person's reasoning, re-evaluate your proposal to see if the comments are worthy. If so, make the necessary changes. You can then move on to other investors, a new proposal, or a new property.

➤   **Appreciation**

People always ask how to evaluate appreciation. The answer is that you don't. Why? Because no one has the ability to predict the future. Properties will typically appreciate in value, but there are no guarantees. While a property that has a high-quality location will usually appreciate the fastest, there are times when property will not appreciate in value, such as during market downturns. If you rely solely on appreciation in your investment proposal, you will be in for a poor return. Most investors will assume that the property will have some appreciation potential, but they won't bet the farm on it.

For example, an investment group had purchased a commercial rental property – a 10,000 square foot facility. When the mortgage interest rates went up, the appreciation of the property went down. In addition, the national chain renting the building started having financial troubles, and they had a twenty-year lease on the property. So the investment group sold the property for very little appreciation value. However, their cash still made a return on the rental income from the property.

That's why smart investors only look at cash on cash return when analyzing proposals. By doing this, you can get a better picture of what your cash will generate in terms of cash returns. Analyzing the investment opportunity in this manner will help you gauge the investment's actual risk/return and will create many more successful experiences for you.

> **Depreciation**

While appreciation assumes the future increase in value of the investment, depreciation assumes how much the base value will diminish. Depreciation is a complex accounting procedure governed by Accounting Principles. In real estate, depreciation cannot be used on land but can be used on the building situated on the land.

Depreciation is based on the principle of "wasting assets." That is, assets get used up over time or have a limited useful life. The logic is that the building will eventually wear down and need to be re-built. Land, on the other hand, will never wear down; it will always be there.

Because of the principles of depreciation, the amount of value in a building that can be depreciated is regulated. In that regard, depreciation of a property becomes intangible because you can't put your hand on it, and it's not "real" money. If the principles change, and they have changed in the past, your returns for a property will also change. Currently in real estate, for income tax purposes, commercial buildings can be depreciated over a thirty-nine year period, while residential buildings are depreciated over twenty-seven and one-half years. The result of this depreciation reduces net income for a property, thus possibly reducing your tax liability.

Before you let your mind race and proclaim that this tax break sounds great, realize that such thinking is precisely what gets most novice investors into trouble. Depreciation is a non-cash expense. Cash requirements for capital items are not related to depreciation.

Depreciation will always be there for you to use in your accounting of the property. Check with your CPA for the latest rules, and always calculate your returns based on cash on cash. As always, stressing potential benefits is the key. So instead of focusing heavily on intangible items such as depreciation, focus instead on the tangible items mentioned earlier.

Combining and analyzing the above tangible and intangible items will provide you with the information you need so you can decide whether to proceed, not to proceed, or re-evaluate the structure of the opportunity, all of which we address in the following chapters.

How Much Money Am I Going to Make?

On page 82 Figure 5a is an example of a blank Preliminary Pro Forma form. Let's first explain each line so you can better understand what investors are looking for.

Figure 5a – Understanding the Preliminary Pro Forma:

Preliminary Pro Forma

Project: A Single Tenant Retail

Budget Item	Cost
1. Property Price	
2. Property Development	
3. Vertical Construction Shell/ with Tenant Specifications	
4. Parking	
5. Architect	
6. Engineer	
7. Permits and Approval Fees	
8. Testing and Inspections	
9. Landscaping	
10. Signage-----In Shell Number	
11. Surveying	
12. Exterior Lighting-----In Shell	
13. Tenant Improvements-----In Shell	
14. Leasing and RE Commissions	
15. Closing and Title Fees	
16. Legal	
17. Financing Fees	
18. Interest	
19. Contingency 5%	
20. Real Estate Taxes- During Construction	

A. Total Project Cost

21. Gross Potential Rents
    Tenant 1-Single Tenant
    Tenant 2
22. Vacancy Factor

23. Effective Gross Rent

24. Debt Service

25. Net Income From Operations
26. Equity Required
27. Cash on Cash Return

Assumptions

Loan Amount
Interest Rate

Debt Service
Rental Rate Year One
Rental Rate Annual Escalations
Operating Expense Pass Through Tenant

Exit Strategy

Total Potential Return

Line One~

Property Price: Fill in the property's current asking price. Later you can alter the purchase price to define your bottom line return and calculate an optimum price required for a successful outcome.

Line Two~

Property Development: This details any land clearing or alterations that may be needed, such as clearing brush or adding fill dirt.

Line Three~

Vertical Shell: If you are constructing a new building, your vertical shell would include the costs associated to construct the foundation, floors, walls, windows, roof, interior plumbing, electrical wiring, and heating and air conditioning. This is separate from the finish work. If you are purchasing an existing structure, this item would be zero, except for any redevelopment costs.

Line Four~

Parking: This details any costs associated with the construction or redevelopment of the parking area.

Line Five~

Architect: List any costs associated with an architect, whether you are building a new structure or redesigning an old.

Line Six~

Engineer: List any costs associated with an engineer, whether you are building a new structure or redesigning an old.

Line Seven~

Permits & Approval Fees: Application fees, building permit fees, and impact fees are examples of charges you face when remodeling or constructing new buildings. Your engineer and architect can help you define these types of fees that are collected by the governmental agencies in your area. You can also visit your local building department for further information on the charges.

Line Eight~

Testing & Inspections: Whether you are constructing a new project, redesigning an old, or purchasing an existing property, you will perform tests and inspections. Geotechnical studies for new development, which test the property's soil conditions; environmental studies, which test for hazardous materials and the presence of any protected species of animal on the property; and engineering studies, which test the condition of an existing structure are a few examples of such tests.

Line Nine~

Landscaping: List the cost of any needed landscaping and irrigation.

Line Ten~

Signage: List the cost associated with any form of building signage required for the property.

Line Eleven~

Surveying: List the cost associated to hire the surveyor. The surveyor will properly identify the property's boundaries.

Line Twelve~

Exterior Lighting: List the cost of repairs or construction of any lighting in the parking areas and along the outside walls of the building.

Line Thirteen~

Tenant Improvements: The objective is to limit any money given to the tenant for improvements, but sometimes it is beneficial for the landlord to provide such improvements as an inducement. Speaking to other landlords and learning what they provide will give you a good idea of the market for tenant improvements (TIs). Items such as carpet, paint, and any other finishings the tenant may need to conduct a successful business excluding furniture, fixtures, and equipment (FF&E) are examples of TIs.

Line Fourteen~

Leasing & Real Estate Commissions: Procuring a tenant for your space will usually cost you leasing and real estate commissions. In some instances you will not use a broker (i.e. if you are a broker with tenant contacts and you are using your commission towards the project fees). Typically, the commission represents seven to ten percent of the net rental income obtained over the full term of your leases. However, it's always best to build this number into your project costs and not get caught off guard.

(Hint: As part of your networking process, seek out brokers who specialize in tenant representation. As with all professionals, their expertise can save you time and money.)

At this point you may be asking, "What if the property is not fully leased prior to the end of the construction period?" First, remember that this is strictly a preliminary form geared to illustrate the property's financial feasibility at the time of lease-up (when the dwelling is available for tenants to take possession of their rented space). Second, if your market studies are such that a full lease-up is not attainable by the time construction is finished, then you will need to add a line item here called "lease-up expense."

By not having the property leased, you will add risk. Your lender may require additional interest to be accounted for, additional equity, or possibly additional principal and interest payments to offset the increased risk. Consult with your lender to uncover the details of their requirements.

Most important is to avoid the "build it and they will come" mentality. Proceed with caution in this situation and re-evaluate your risk. Consult with a real estate professional versed in the market and in tenant representation. Re-evaluate your market studies. Look specifically at the competition for your product. Ask questions like: "Are their enough end users looking for space?" "Are there more end users than space available?" "What is the vacancy of existing competition?" When you momentarily step back to check the facts, you will thrive.

Line Fifteen~

Closing & Title Fees: List the costs associated with the closing and title work. Your attorney or title company can estimate this number based on the state in which your property lies and the purchase or selling price of your property.

Line Sixteen~

Legal: List the attorney fees paid for closing the property and reviewing contracts and leases. Present your attorney with the scope of work and ask for an estimate.

Line Seventeen~

Financing Fees: Your lender may charge points on the mortgage as well as other fees associated with the preparation of the note. You can obtain an estimate of these costs from your lender. These fees vary depending upon the lender, the market, and the size of the loan.

Line Eighteen~

Interest During Construction: Most construction loans are short term. The payments on these loans are interest only payments charged during the construction period. Permanent financing after construction requires a principal and interest payment. Your lender will provide you the interest due on your loan.

Line Nineteen~

Contingency: Contingency costs are typically estimated at three to five percent of the total project cost. Having a contingency in your project costs will help you offset any unforeseen expenses. By doing your homework upfront you can alleviate the need to dip into this item. However, in the real world it's often necessary. So don't be caught off guard; prepare for it here.

Line Twenty~

Real Estate Taxes: List any governmental taxes associated with the project.

Line A~

Total Cost of Project: Add lines one through twenty.

Line Twenty-One~

Gross Potential Rents: If you are purchasing an existing property, this will be the rental income you would receive on an annual basis. If it is new construction, then this would be the income potential of the property based on your earlier market studies.

Line Twenty-Two ~

Vacancy Factor: List the vacancy percentage you anticipate. Most people figure this at ten percent, unless you have a single tenant property. Then, of course, you would have no vacancy factor. Multiplying the vacancy percentage (.10 for a 10% vacancy factor) by your gross rents will give you the vacancy number to plug into the form.

Line Twenty-Three -

Effective Gross Rent: This is the amount on line twenty-one (Gross Potential Rents) minus the amount on line twenty-two (Vacancy Factor). This may sound like an easy item to figure, but don't forget to consider your operating expenses – such things as real estate taxes, landscaping upkeep, and janitorial services. These items are typically passed through (billed separately) to the tenant on a prorata basis.

For example, if you have a 10,000 square foot building and a tenant rents 5,000 square feet, then this tenant's prorata share would be fifty percent. Thus, the tenant would receive a bill from the landlord for fifty percent of the operating expenses. Some landlords separate the operating expenses out when leasing the space and others simply include it into the rental rate. Whether you separate or include depends upon your market and the way you'd like to present the property to the tenant. Whatever you choose, you must know what the numbers are so you can calculate a bottom line net rental number as shown.

If you choose to include operating expenses as part of the rent that the tenant will pay and not a separate billing item, then you will need to create a line item here called "operating expenses." Your next step will be to subtract your operating expenses from the effective gross rent. For the purposes of this example it is being separated out and is considered a full pass-through to the tenants.

Note: Operating expenses are quite different from capital improvements made to the property. Capital improvements are items such as a new parking lot or driveway, a new roof, a building remodel, etc. These expenses cannot be included in the operating costs passed through to the tenants. However, these are costs that you must include in your property analysis. A good rule of thumb in distinguishing capital expenses from operating expenses is that capital expenses can be depreciated.

Line Twenty-Four-

Debt Service: List your principal and interest payments. You can obtain this information from the amortization schedule your lender provided.

Line Twenty-Five-

Net Income From Operations: This is the amount on line twenty-three (Effective Gross Rents) minus the amount on line twenty-four (Debt Service). It shows your income potential.

Line Twenty-Six-

Equity Required: This is the difference between the cost of the project (Line A) and the loan amount in the Assumptions Box. It shows how much cash you'll need to proceed.

Line Twenty-Seven-

Cash on Cash Return (coc): This is calculated as line twenty-five (net income from operations) divided by line twenty-six (equity required). In our example of a successful preliminary plan, (Figure 5b) you get .12581, a decimal number that you can express as a percentage by multiplying it by 100, giving you a 12.581% or 12.58% return. In analyzing the cash on cash return number, you can compare it to other investment opportunities. For example, if an investor can purchase a bank CD and get a five percent safe return, and your cash on cash return is five or even six or seven percent, you can safely say that your project should be scrapped or your numbers re-evaluated. If you have met with the property owner and he or she appears to be very inflexible with the purchase price, then you may want to simply move on or make another offer to see if it will get you anywhere. To determine the purchase price number that works for you, just plug in new price numbers in the form to see what happens to the other figures. (Refer to chapter six for tips and pointers on getting to that number with the owner.)

Can I Trust the Numbers?

The two example pro formas (figure 5b and figure 5c) are for the same property. The difference is that the purchase price of the land changed (line one), as did the tenant's rental rate (line twenty-one). The financing changed too, but only in the amount of the required down payment. While a fifteen percent down payment was used in both options, fifteen percent of $2,113,075 (Total Project Cost on Line A) is much greater than fifteen percent of $1,863,075. That alone changed the return numbers.

The rate that a potential buyer is willing to pay as a function of the purchase price is 8.75% in both cases, but because the rental income for the property went down in the second example, so did the percent of return. The risk on the second example was simply too large to undertake. The "possible solutions" section of the second example shows what could remedy the situation.

Figure 5b - An Accepted Preliminary Pro Forma:

Below is an example of a preliminary pro forma that was accepted and in which the project went forward.

Preliminary Pro Forma

Project: A Single Tenant Retail

Budget Item	Cost
1. Property Price	$850,000
2. Property Development	65,000
3. Vertical Construction Shell with Tenant Specifications	580,000
4. Parking	70,000
5. Architect	10,000
6. Engineer	15,000
7. Permits and approval fees	68,000
8. Testing and Inspections	6,000
9. Landscaping	14,000
10. Signage-----in shell number	0
11. Surveying	3,000
12. Exterior lighting-----in shell	0
13. Tenant Improvements-----in shell	0
14. Leasing and RE Commissions	78,000
15. Closing and title fees	13,200
16. Legal	7,000
17. Financing Fees	13,875
18. Interest	38,000
19. Contingency 5%	27,000
20. Real Estate Taxes-construction	5,000
A. Total Project Cost	**$1,863,075**

21. Gross potential rents 11,000sf Tenant 1-Single Tenant Tenant 2	$203,500
22. Vacancy Factor	0
23. Effective Gross Rent	203,500
24. Debt Service	165,756
25. Net Income From Operations	**37,743**
26. Equity Required	**300,000**
27. Cash on Cash Return	**13%**

Assumptions

Loan Amount	1,563,075
Interest Rate	8.75%
Debt Service	165,756
Rental Rate Year One	18.50
Rental Rate Annual Escalations.	2%
Operating Expense Pass Through Tenant	

Exit Strategy

Potential Buyers will pay $2,400,000.
Sell at start of lease.

Total Potential Return

$2,400,000 less $1,863,075, approximately $500,000 less some closing expense

170% return on investment of $300,000.00

If no, hold at13% Cash on Cash Return.
CDs at 5%.

Proceed

Figure 5c ~ Preliminary Pro Forma to be Re-Evaluated:

Below is an example of a preliminary pro forma that was rejected and in which the project was re-evaluated.

Preliminary Pro Forma

Project: A Single Tenant Retail

Budget Item	Cost
1. Property Price	$1,100,000
2. Property Development	65,000
3. Vertical Construction Shell with Tenant Specifications	580,000
4. Parking	70,000
5. Architect	10,000
6. Engineer	15,000
7. Permits and approval fees	68,000
8. Testing and Inspections	6,000
9. Landscaping	14,000
10. Signage-----in shell number	0
11. Surveying	3,000
12. Exterior lighting-----in shell	0
13. Tenant Improvements-----in shell	0
14. Leasing and RE Commissions	78,000
15. Closing and title fees	13,200
16. Legal	7,000
17. Financing Fees	13,875
18. Interest	38,000
19. Contingency 5%	27,000
20. Real Estate Taxes-construction	5,000
A. Total Project Cost	$2,113,075

21. Gross potential rents 11,000sf Tenant 1-Single Tenant Tenant 2	$187,000
22. Vacancy Factor	0
23. Effective Gross Rent	187,000
24. Debt Service	190,469
25. Net Income From Operations	3,500
26. Equity Required	316,961
27. Cash on Cash Return	1%

Assumptions

Loan Amount	1,796,114
Interest Rate	8.75%
Debt Service	165,756
Rental Rate Year One	17
Rental Rate Annual Escalations.	2%
Operating Expense Pass Through Tenant	

Exit Strategy

Potential Buyers will pay $2,200,000.
Sell at start of lease.
Market is soft. Properties are not selling.

Total Potential Return
$2,400,000 less $2,113,075, approximately $140,000 less some closing expense
(Any cost overruns can reduce this return significantly.)

44% return on investment of $316,961.00

If no sale 1%, is unacceptable.

Pass or Re-negotiate for Better Returns.

Possible Solutions ➢
• Obtain higher rents from tenant.
• Lower purchase price from landlord.
• Get better rate from lender.
• Lock in purchaser prior to firm commitment to limit risk of hold at 1%.

Note: CD rates are currently 5%.
➢ If Buyer puts $500,000 down and can obtain an 8.5% interest rate loan on the balance, this then creates a 4% Cash on Cash Return.

➢ If Buyer puts $1,000,000 down and can obtain an 8.0% interest rate loan on the balance, this then creates an 11% Cash on Cash Return.

Conclusion ➢
A Large Cash Buyer or a Section 1031 Tax Deffered Exchange Buyer is required.

The Profit Pro Forma & Beyond

The pro forma plan is nothing more than the addition of all the expenses you can possibly encounter in the project compared to the income the project can generate. Rest assured that your preliminary plan will be the basis to your final plan, and you will not have to recreate many of these figures at the end phase. With your preliminary plan, you have the makings to the final proposal in your hands.

Tweaking the numbers and placing the actual numbers into the form will get you to the finish line. Remember that these numbers are for your evaluation only; therefore, your objectivity here is crucial so you don't make an emotional purchase. Listen to your numbers. As the numbers change, so too should your negotiating tactics. Walk away if the numbers don't stack up. Remember time is money, so work only on properties that will produce a successful outcome.

Most people who are not accustomed to using this type of financial analysis initially think doing one is a waste of time. However, without fail, whenever one of these doubters tries using this form to analyze a property, he or she is instantly hooked and won't even consider a property without using this very valuable tool.

This tool is now being passed on to you. So use it. Make your decisions with lightning fast speed—that's the purpose of a preliminary plan. The numbers don't lie; trust them and keep your emotions clear. Use this valuable tool to evaluate all your properties.

Regardless of the response your proposal receives, remember that everyone is on your side. The investors want to make money on their money. The vendors want more business from you. The seller wants to sell the property. You are presenting everyone with a potentially great opportunity.

Do you want the success that the end result will bring? Of course you do. Are the rewards worth the time? They Are, So Go For It!

> Take time to understand and work the numbers.

Chapter Five:
Anchoring Ideas – An Exercise

Get People
On Your Side

As you build your preliminary pro forma, continue to build your network database.

1.   Take a few bankers to lunch individually or sit with them for an hour to discuss their lending criteria.

Ask such questions as:

> ➤   "How do you underwrite a loan?" (This is their lending criterion.)

> ➤   "What percentage of equity do you look for in properties?"

> ➤   "What types of properties do you have an appetite for?"

> ➤   "How do you measure risk?"

> ➤   "What types of personal guarantees do you want?"

> ➤   "If I were to provide a detailed plan and investment proposal, would you know investors who would be interested?"

> ➤   "What are your interest rates?"

The purpose of this is to build rapport so the bankers know who you are when you call, and so that they actually take your call.

You are a real person, and so are they. Once they see the professional package that you put together, you will have their attention. Remember to be factual and thorough.

(Hint: If you feel that the conversation is not working, be polite while you are there, but then move on to another banker. This particular person may not be right for your personality type. Find someone else who you click with. Remember, you are going to be working with this person. If you can't even have lunch with him or her, then don't go further into a transaction.)

2.   Review your territory.

Drive around and look for anything new. Start filling in the preliminary pro forma and information package on a property that you believe has the most potential, given your current information. Analyze the property to see if it is worth pursuing based on the knowledge you have learned.

You Can Do It!
Find out what it's worth to you.

Chapter Six ~

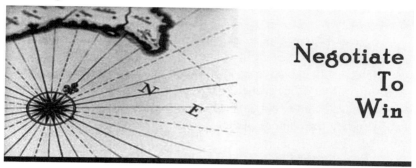

Negotiate To Win

Now that you have decided to go forward with your property and have the basis for commercial real estate success, it's time to put those skills to work by getting the property under contract and negotiating the best deal. This is the point where it all comes down to you. If you've done your homework and diligently worked the exercises up to this point, you will succeed. This chapter and the next two will add to your arsenal.

Negotiation is ongoing in any commercial real estate transaction. It occurs before, during, and especially after a contract presentation. As you negotiate with the other party, always remind yourself that everything you want in regards to the transaction is currently in the hands of someone else. Whether you're buying or selling, this concept holds true. On the buying side, someone else has the property that you want. When selling, someone else has the money that you want for the property. Therefore, the key to any great negotiation, whether buying or selling, is mastering the ability to get what you want from the other party while making them happy that they gave it to you for a fair price.

The Price Paid for Winning at All Costs

Back in the 1700s and early 1800s, the way to motivate people was to take them out for a good thrashing – a "flogging" if you will. People believed that this was the best way to "encourage" others to do what they wanted them to do.

While it's nice to believe that our mentality has evolved since then, quite the opposite is true. Many people still think that negotiation meetings should be like a boxing match: The two sides continually go after each other until one gives in and loses. The victor then parades around the ring proclaiming to be "the best in the world."

Consider the typical negotiation scene we commonly see in the movies. The meeting takes place in a huge mahogany wood boardroom large enough to seat twenty-five people at the conference table and another twenty-five around the perimeter. Bigwig attorneys try to intimidate each other as they "hammer out the deal." There's a lot of money on the line, huge attorney fees, and a predominance of scare tactics designed to wear the other side out.

How can anyone think straight with that kind of pressure? The answer is: **You Can't!** That's why such negotiation meetings usually fail miserably.

Four Traits of a Deal Maker

True negotiation is about winning people over, not tiring them out. In fact, there are four special qualities all successful negotiators possess, and they all involve having the ability to work with, not against, the other side.

Great Negotiators are:
1. Genuinely interested in others.
2. Genuinely happy and show it.
3. Excellent listeners.
4. Interested in having others talk about themselves.

When you work with others to create "win-win" solutions, you'll close more contracts in less time. And the more you exude these four traits, the quicker you'll get the other side to relax and actually *want* to negotiate with you. Let me share with you an example of this negotiation style in action.

About 15 years ago, a young man named Mark wanted a meeting to discuss leasing space in a property that I had available for rent. The meeting was to take place at his office with his boss, who was the owner of Mark's company.

When the day arrived, I met Mark in the lobby. He appeared to be nervous, jittery, and a bit hyper. He buzzed from one side of the lobby to another, stopping to "prep" me for the meeting with the "big man."

"The boss doesn't have any time for small talk," Mark cautioned. "He will cut you off when he wants. He won't listen. He is very tough and he will eat you alive. He is an ex-star football player, so he's got this big office and a huge ego to match."

Mark went on and on and on. Finally, the secretary interrupted and showed us into the "big man's" office.

Mark was right; the office was huge, filled with trophies and football memorabilia. To my surprise, a golf trophy sat prominently on the desk.

The "big man" sat behind his desk. I walked over to his desk with a big smile on my face, extended my hand, greeted him cheerfully, and then commented on the wonderful golf trophy, not his football ones.

The "big man" introduced himself as George and spoke for the next five minutes about golf. He asked me if I played. I responded affirmatively and mentioned a few people that he might know of in the golfing circles. This spurred George to speak for the next fifteen minutes. As George was speaking, I just happened to catch a glimpse of Mark out of the corner of my eye and noticed his mouth hanging open.

George then turned the conversation to the lease by talking about his business. He was trying to sell me on the value his business would bring to the property. Mark tried to speak a couple of times, but the "big man" stifled him. We finished the lease in the next few days. As you can guess, George wouldn't allow Mark to do anything to the lease other than deliver the signed document to our office.

The moral: You will always get what you need if you allow the other party to do all the talking. Sit back and listen, and they will tell you exactly what needs to happen to get the transaction done. By simply asking a few questions and employing the four qualities above, you will be awesome.

Specific Steps for Sealing the Deal

Now that you know the attitude you must exude in order to negotiate successfully, it's time to learn the precise "tactics" that will lead to a productive outcome. If you want to achieve favorable results during a negotiation, put the following negotiation strategies to work.

➤ 1. Know What You Want and What You Will Accept

Prior to any negotiation, clearly define all the terms that you are willing to accept and the conditions under which you will accept them. You have been building the preliminary pro forma to give you that picture, so use it. Keep these terms specific, yet be flexible to changes. Once you have a clear definition of your essential terms, you can progress your negotiating strategy from there, knowing that the negotiation will better your position and terms. When you neglect this step, you often enter negotiations with a sense of indifference. The other party will sense your uncertainty and won't take you or your contract demands seriously. That's why it's important to stay off the fence and state your position upfront.

➤2. Make a Realistic Offer

There are both good and bad ways to achieve the terms you want in a negotiation. Some investors think coming in with a ridiculous lowball offer is the best strategy. They hope that by presenting an extremely low offer, the other party will negotiate to raise the offer while bringing the original asking price or terms down. This is a miserable way to negotiate, as it alienates the seller. Instead, savvy investors build a reputation of being a fair player. They know that consistently giving unrealistic offers makes them appear less than honorable and that doing so will limit the number of contracts they are able to close.

After giving a lowball offer, it's very possible that the seller will refuse to counter your offer. It's also possible that the property owner will not let you raise your initial offer. He or she may automatically assume that you're an amateur and may choose not to work with you at all. That's why the lowball approach can cause you to lose more properties than it's worth.

There may be an instance when you think the offering price is completely unrealistic and you feel justified in making a lowball offer. If you ever find yourself in that situation, don't do it. Instead, meet with the property owner and share your market studies and comparable sales figures with him or her. Reiterate your interest in the property. Let the owner know that he or she has a good piece of property, but there are still some obstacles you have to overcome. Share the fact that based on this information you cannot pay the asking price at this time. Then, stop talking and sit back and listen. You may find an opening for compromise.

If, however, the door closes on the owner's part, don't give up. Offer to leave the information you have so he or she can review it in private. Let the owner know that you are always open to discussing the property. Ask if you can contact the owner in a few days after he or she has had time to think it over. Your attempt here is to open a door for further discussions. You want the owner to trust you and talk openly with you about all the selling requirements, not simply the price. And by all means, follow up.

If you're selling and you get a lowball offer, don't even respond. The person is most likely not a serious buyer. Ignore the offer so you don't encourage this type of negotiating.

➤3.   Listen to the Other Party's Feedback

As the other party responds to your contract requests, ask questions and listen to the answers. Some great questions to ask are: "What are your concerns with these requests?" "Which areas do you feel are unreasonable and why?" "Which points are you comfortable with and why?" Remember, asking and listening are important because you will always get what you want if you allow the other party to do the talking. You simply have to act on what they say.

➤4.   Don't Make it a Price Negotiation

During a negotiation, "slick talking" brokers often say something like: "What's it going to take to get this deal done?" or "Where are we on price?" They try to get to the bottom line much too quickly. However, when price becomes the only issue, you limit your negotiation options, give the other party the impression that "this is my best offer; take it or leave it," and set up a situation in which there will be a winner and a loser. Knowing that we all hate to lose, your negotiations will end abruptly.

Here's the best strategy: Meet with the property owner. Let him or her know that you have looked at the property. Share some due diligence information with the owner, such as demographic information and the aerial photographs. Share enough to show that you are serious about the property. Point out the good and the bad about the property. Then, when it comes time to offer the price, say something like, *"Based on the pro forma plan we have done given the data we have to date, we like your property but at this time it looks as though we can only pay around _____ dollars for it."* The important point is to use the phrases "to date," "at this time," and "around ____ dollars." Why? You want to leave room for movement. If you make it sound as if your price is set in stone, then it's probably the end of the negotiations. You have also left the data window open.

Taking it a step further, be sure to stress other important factors during your negotiation, such as closing dates, inspection time frames, etc. You can then use these other factors to move the transaction forward. When people understand all that will happen in their favor, the final price won't be so much of an issue.

➤5.   Rely on Yourself; Not on Luck

Regardless of what happens during a negotiation session, luck has absolutely no bearing on the outcome. **Luck is simply the moment when opportunity and preparation meet.** If you take your time and master the art of data gathering, of knowing your location inside and out, and of conducting objective risk analysis, then you will always close the deal to meet everyone's needs.

➤6.   Be a Problem Solver

People instinctively move towards things that give them pleasure and away from the things that cause them pain. The person you are negotiating with wants to take actions that result in happiness. If you are gaining pleasure from the negotiation but your terms are causing pain to the other party, it is going to be a frustrating negotiation, and you are probably not going to get what you want. Therefore, you must uncover what pleasure the other party wants to gain as a result of your transaction. If you encounter indifference, then it's time to walk away, because you will spin your wheels forever. Outright opposition is better, as it tells you exactly where the pleasure and pain are and how to make the deal happen. At that point, you will know what you need to do to create a win-win situation, and then you can build on it. One way to do this is a trade off play, where you offer a concession. You could say, "I may be willing to do _____ for you, but what would you be willing to do for me in return?" You are essentially saying, "I'll give you some pleasure if you give me some pleasure." You can now solve the other person's problem while you get what you want.

➤7.   Observe Body Language

Watching the movements of the other party can disclose a great deal about the words that they say. For example, if they are unable to look at you when they are talking, then they could be hiding something. If they are fidgeting in the chair, they could be very uncomfortable. If they sit back and fold their arms, they could be tuning you out. If they are sitting forward on the edge of their chair, they may be eager to hear more. You can also use your body language to communicate to your partner in a transaction. So if you feel the negotiation is going poorly, you can both agree to call it quits with the other party without ever speaking a word to each other.

➤8.   Believe in Co-Authorship to Win

One of the best strategies for negotiating is to get everyone involved in authorship of the contract together. To start a negotiation by saying, "This is our standard contract and we must use it," sets up a tough negotiation session. A better approach is to offer to start with your standard contract to get things going and then allow for a follow-up discussion on any changes the other party wishes to make. Also, during negotiations it's often advantageous to offer something to the other party so you can build trust. For example, you could ask if they would like to start with *their* standard contract for you to review. Failure to get everyone's input upfront may kill the deal at the starting block.

➤9.   Keep Your Options Open ... Always

Realize that people do not all want the same thing. You cannot assume, for example, that the seller wants to sell because he or she wants the money. There are many different reasons why people want to sell. Once you discover the real reason, you may opt to completely change your negotiation strategy.

   For example, a 75-year old man wanted to sell his property. Most people assumed that he wanted to sell simply because he needed the money. In reality, he didn't need to sell for financial reasons. Rather, he wanted to put all of his money into Treasury Bills. He felt that his heirs would not be able to successfully manage the property to create the return on investment that he could obtain. Money was not his motivator. He wanted to line up his estate for his heirs before he died, making it simple for them to handle.

Incorporate all the previous steps into every negotiation session you participate in.

The Outcome Will Amaze You!

The Three-Meeting Strategy

When I first started in the real estate business, I developed a plan called the Three-Meeting Tactic. I did this for one reason only: I did not have a lot of experience in judging the transaction. I understood that time was money, so I did not want to waste my time on any one transaction. I needed to develop my skills. If I wasn't in the deal by the third meeting, I moved on.

As I became more experienced, I realized that this approach needed modification and that transactions sometimes take longer. But for someone just starting, this strategy can help you develop the skills you need to move through the transaction successfully. As you gain experience, you may very well phase this approach out of your negotiation sessions, but it's a great starting point for real estate newcomers.

> ➤   The First Meeting-

> In the first meeting, it is very important for you to hear what the other party wants and needs, even if you are not interested. You want to establish communication and trust, and discover a common element you both share.
>
> For example, many years ago I conducted a transaction that involved an industrial piece of property of approximately 20 acres, for which my sellers were asking $650,000. The year was 1980, and in those days that was a significant price for the property. The perfect buyer for the property was the surrounding property owner. He had created an industrial park around the land, and this was the one piece that he had not been able to acquire. Located in the middle of his development, the property had frontage to another road that could give him a great link to the rest of the park.

The interested buyer felt he deserved this piece of property at a very low price, and that was his only stated requirement. My primary concern during this first meeting was to find out what he really wanted – what he wasn't revealing currently. I already knew that he would say the property was of no value to any other buyer and that we should sell it for half the $650,000 asking price. I listened to him without interrupting so I could establish lines of communication. I also wanted to find some common ground. I found the common ground by looking around his office. I noticed that he was an avid golfer, so I started a conversation about golf. For the next thirty minutes, we discussed the sport.

With the lines of communication established, I was able to leverage the seller's power. As we moved into the business discussion, I listed all the benefits the buyer would receive by purchasing the property at the asking price. I then informed him that the seller and his partnership only agreed to sell the property at the listing price. I further mentioned that there were a number of other items we could discuss to make this transaction happen.

I then asked to see drawings of the entire industrial development, because I knew it would help significantly in communicating to my sellers how the park would be set up and how this property would fit in with the buyer's plan. I used this as a trigger to talk about the benefits to him once again, reminding him that there were other buyers in the area that would love to be in this location.

At that point we could not go any further with the negotiations until I spoke with my sellers to find out how much they wanted to compromise. I revealed that I could not speak for my client, and that he and I needed to meet again. I also cordially threw out the invitation to play golf sometime.

Back at the office, I updated my sellers on the negotiation proceedings and prepared them for the fact that this was the right buyer for the property. I explained that he would close under any circumstances because he was motivated, whereas other buyers may just tie up the property while they are considering the purchase, and then not do anything.

The Second Meeting~

In the second meeting the goal is to work towards a compromise, but not settle on a decision. This is when you ask additional questions about what the other party expects and which items are important in the contract from the opposing party's point of view. That gives you the opportunity to hear about the buyer's needs, such as "I need more financing," "I need more time to figure out the property," or "I need more architectural drawings."

In the second meeting with the prospective purchaser mentioned previously, I met the potential buyer's project manager, who had prepared a possible plan for the property. In an attempt to show that the property was of no value to anyone else and of some value to him, he produced a plan that showed a large driveway with one or two small buildings next to it. He felt that this proved his point and that he should get the property for half the asking price.

Knowing the current property owner, I was confident that such an offer would never fly. In order to keep the lines of communication open, I knew I had to speak the truth to the potential buyer. I quickly informed him that this proposal would go nowhere. The owner would only sell the property for the listed price. He didn't *need* to sell.

I then reinforced my position by stating that I wanted to sell the property, and that if he was not going to buy it for the asking price, then I would find someone else who would. I further explained why it would be a mistake for him not to purchase the property, and I reiterated all the benefits he would receive as a result of owning the property. I even shared my thoughts on how he could increase the rents he charged simply by gaining access to the road the property provided.

The potential for more money in his pocket caught his attention, so I continued on that path. I informed him that he could save money on the project by carefully structuring the timing of the closing. Plus, by not requiring him to close soon and granting him time to conduct feasibility studies and obtain permits, we limited his risk and saved him interest on the project. (In reality, the buyer probably already knew these factors, but by bringing those items into the open, I let him know that we were educated sellers and understood his position.)

I concluded by saying that we could negotiate other terms to make the purchase happen. We then discussed a few optional terms. The potential buyer finished by stating that he needed some time to think things over. We scheduled our third and final meeting for the following week.

The Third Meeting-

The third meeting (a.k.a. the pressure meeting) puts all the weight on your shoulders to either move the potential transaction forward or to leave it and move on. This is usually your last chance to "get into the deal," so the goal is to get the purchase offer started. During the third meeting you should be able to solve many items and begin the purchase contract. One way to get started is to end the meeting with an offer to prepare a preliminary purchase contract for the other party's review. Once you receive an affirmation to start, you are officially in the transaction. It now becomes a matter of applying the nine skills in this chapter.

If, on the other hand, you do not receive confirmation to start, you may want to walk away from the transaction and possibly revisit it later. This will keep you from spinning your wheels and wasting time with something that may not happen.

For the buyer in this example's case, the third meeting proved to be the deal closer. When we met, we discussed our golf games for thirty minutes and promised each other that no matter what happened in this transaction we would play a round of golf. I then met again with his project manager to review the details of the property and to discuss terms in which he could purchase the property. The price never came up again, and we closed the transaction.

You Can Get What You Want

Realize that the negotiation guidelines in this chapter are just that – guidelines. There is no one "right" way to negotiate. As you master the techniques in this book, you will develop your own style of negotiating. The more you practice that style, the better results you'll obtain.

But remember that negotiation is just one piece of the puzzle. Learn from the results you get, and then adjust your tactics until you receive the outcome you really want.

> Only when you master the entire package of skills will you reach your goals.

Anchoring Ideas ~ An Exercise

A Different
Way To Get
What You Want

Practice your negotiating skills.

You can apply these negotiating techiques to any part of your life. A great place to start is with your own family.

Would you like to develop a better relationship with particular family members? By using the four negotiation qualities, you can. First, become genuinely interested in your family members. Ask them to talk about their day. Be happy and encouraging as they speak. Don't interrupt them; just listen. Practice getting them to talk about their experiences.

If you master this exercise with your family, you will automatically carry the qualities over into your business life and you will become a great negotiator.

Try it; the other person will appreciate you more than you ever imagined.

What Do You Have to Lose?

Chapter Seven ~

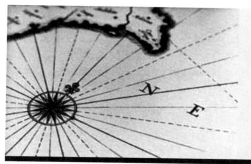

Gain Control Without Getting Bitten

Provided that your preliminary pro forma sheet was positive, your objective now is to get the property under contract. You want to gain control long enough to complete the investment analysis form and put the remaining pieces of the transaction together.

Now you are serious. Real money is on the line and being spent on your property studies and inspections. You are hiring engineers to perform property investigations. You are hiring architects to re-design the property. You are talking to potential tenants. You are finalizing the pro forma plan and meeting with your investors. You are finalizing banking relations. It's an exciting time because a lot is happening all at once. It may seem helter-skelter, but let's look at the events in this process.

(Hint: The following list is in a logical order; however, your individual circumstances may require you to do certain steps out of order.)

➤1.   **Secure your capital.**

In every project you will need three types of capital or equity to make the transaction happen. The first is called "seed" capital. It is the initial money required to start (seed) the transaction. In the example in the introduction of this book, the $5,000 deposit my friend provided is an example of seed capital.

Seed capital is the most risky money because it is invested prior to having all the information. Since it is the most risky capital, it holds the highest return. Seed capital consists of the deposit money required by the purchase contract, and any funds required by engineers and other vendors to study the property.

The second form of capital is called equity. It represents the remaining balance of money required above the mortgage loan. The third form of capital is the debt financing, or the mortgage loan.

➤2.   **Get the property under contract.**

At this stage many people ask to see a sample purchase contract. You will not find one in this book, because when dealing with real estate investments worth hundreds of thousands and possibly even millions of dollars it's imperative that you hire an attorney versed in real estate law to prepare the purchase and sale contract.

Some real estate brokers will suggest that you use a form contract provided by the local Board of Realtors rather than spend money for an attorney. This is wrong and misleading advice. The only time it's acceptable to use a form contract is when you're buying or selling a single family home. If you do decide to use a form contract for your commercial real estate transactions (despite the advice not to), at least have a real estate attorney review all the documents before you sign them. The attorney works for you and has your best interests in mind, so you can be sure the contract is a solid one that protects you.

Each contract contains specialized items based on the transaction itself. After all, you are working with a different property, a different seller, or a different buyer every time. Therefore, each transaction will have its own needs. When working in commercial real estate, there's really no way to satisfy every person and every situation with a standard form contract. Remember to stand out from the crowd and keep building good habits. Most real estate agents are not well versed in contract law, so don't cut corners here. It is simply not worth the risk. Hire an attorney and familiarize yourself with the specific contract items found later in this chapter. Doing so will strengthen your position.

➤3.   **Hire professionals to get the right answers.**

You are still seeking answers to the property's suitability for you and identifying exactly what you have. Hire the right engineers, architects, and geotechnical engineers to give you the answers you need to make a logical decision. Also talk with potential tenants to determine the end user's interest in the property.

➤4.   **Fill in the blanks to your pro forma.**

As you complete these steps, continue finalizing your pro forma and investment plan. Chapter eight gives more details on finalizing your documents.

➤5.   **Meet with your lender.**

Keep your lender updated on the project status. He or she will be able to give you final loan requirements as the project moves closer to reality.

➤6.   **Re-visit with your potential investors.**

Keep your investors updated on the project status. Conduct a final investment plan meeting so you can officially bring them into your project. They are the final equity requirement for the project, so sign them up as soon as possible.

➤7.   **Apply for the loan.**

Fill out any necessary forms your lender provides, and have your attorney review the documents for accuracy.

➤8.   **Manage any professional that is performing work for you.**

Make sure all your hired professionals are staying on their timelines and that they understand the full scope of their project.

➤9.   **Check your contract timing.**

Successful real estate professionals are on top of things. Check your calendar to see if you are due for any additional deposits and to verify that you are still in the inspection time period. Make sure any items you are supposed to have completed are done.

➢10.   **Meet with tenants and/or prospective tenants.**

If the property currently has tenants, meet with them so you can gain an understanding of the lease in existence. Are they coming up for lease renewal? If so, what are their intentions? Are they renewing? If no, then go back to the seller with this issue, as it greatly affects your pro forma and may cause you to kill the deal. If you are meeting with new tenants, then you will want to sign them up as quickly as possible. Start the lease negotiations immediately.

➢11.   **Meet with the professionals for final information on the property.**

Ask the professionals you hire to provide you with a detailed report of their findings. If anyone has uncovered any potential problems, deal with those items immediately.

➢12.   **Meet with any governmental authorities.**

Your engineers and architects can guide you in this process and inform you of which agencies you'll need to confer with.

➢13.   **Contact your lender and title company as to the progress of the loan.**

Make sure things are progressing as planned. Always ask if there is anything you can do to speed up the process.

➢14.   **Follow up with any prospective tenants.**

Ask how their lease review process is going and find out if there is anything you can do to speed up the process.

➢15.   **Review any title issues that the lender or the title company may have "flagged" with your attorney.**

If anything seems irregular, your lender or title company may kill the deal for you. Uncover such items as soon as possible and get them resolved immediately.

➤16.   **Recheck your contract timing.**

Are any materials due, such as a survey? Are any deposit monies entering the non-refundable stage? Is the end of your inspection time period drawing near?

If all inspections and other problems are resolved to your satisfaction, then proceed with the project. If not, then discuss your concerns with the seller and rewrite the contract to create time to satisfy the items. Remember, you will have to negotiate to win.

Continue working in this manner and you are sure to succeed while you limit your risk in the project and make your investors very happy. By keeping your investors satisfied you will have a captive audience for the next property. That's when the business becomes a lot easier. Your strong network will be in place and working for you.

Protect Yourself with High-Powered Contract Clauses

A big part of gaining control is getting the contract you want. As you buy and sell more properties, you'll use and see many different contract clauses. Below are some of the more important ones you should strive to put into each of your contracts. If you cannot end up with them in your contract, it may be a good negotiation starting point. Sometimes you may end up with some of these clauses watered down from their original version. In that case you have done great to get some portion of these clauses into your contract.

Power Clause One–
Contingency of Inspection & Approval Prior to Closing.

As the buyer, you should be able to inspect and approve the condition of the property. After all, what if the property becomes in disrepair while you are in contract because of the owner's negligence? Or, what if the property has some hidden defect that only a thorough inspection would reveal? You need this protection in your contract. If you are purchasing a commercial property, especially a piece of vacant land, use wording such as the following:

Purchaser shall have a period of Sixty (Ninety or One Hundred Twenty, whichever is appropriate for the situation) days to conduct a feasibility study of the property to determine if the property is suitable for the buyer's intended use.

You can then go on to describe the information you are going to gather in that period of time. For land, you will perform soil tests and environmental studies. For commercial or residential income property, you will review all leases and perform building and environmental studies to make sure there are no hidden expenses. If you discover that the property is not suitable for your investment criteria after you have done this additional research, you can negotiate with the seller for more time, request that the seller make the repairs at the seller's cost, or cancel the contract and receive a refund of your deposit money.

Here are some examples of what you should be looking for during this phase.

> ➢ **The size of the usable property, as that is the real value.**

> For example, a few years ago I was involved with the purchase of a vacant piece of land. The seller assured me that the property was in good condition and did not have any problems or environmental issues. However, when I asked for time to conduct my feasibility study, he hesitated. I informed the seller that I would not be willing to take on that kind of risk for my investors or myself. I further explained that if he could not grant me the time to conduct a feasibility study, then I would not be able to purchase his property.

> After some consideration and time (two months, to be exact), the seller approached me and asked if I was still interested. I told him that I was, but only if he had changed his mind regarding the feasibility study. He had. With that, I agreed to keep all the terms of the contract the same as they were two months earlier.

> Was my stubbornness for this clause warranted? You bet. Further investigation showed that there were issues with wetland on the property, which greatly reduced the size of the usable property. There were also soil problems that significantly added to the cost of the project. It soon became obvious that there was a lot more work needed in structuring this transaction to meet my investment criteria. Fortunately, we weren't committed to the property thanks to the inspection clause.

➤   **The property's soil conditions.**

In Florida, for example, the land is located at a low altitude and is typically swampland, or has been at one time. So it's important for buyers to conduct extensive soil boring tests so they can find out what makes up the base of the soil underneath the land they are purchasing. The best approach is to hire geotechnical engineers who drive augers into the soil at different spots on the property, typically where the building will sit, and pull soil samples. One of the things buyers look for in Florida is whether the soil base is muck. In the north, it may be a rock base. If the base is muck, which is a very unstable soil, it will cost the buyer a significant amount of money to "demuck" the area. This process will add to the development costs of your raw land.

Realize, though, that such tests aren't infallible. In one feasibility study we commissioned, the geographic engineer conducted borings under the site of the planned building, spaced every twenty to thirty feet. The results showed no muck and a good soil base, so we purchased the property. When we started digging where the building would be situated, we discovered a huge muck field meandering around the soil borings. This deep muck area added about $150,000 in costs.

This left us with two options. We could either clean out the muck or re-design the site plan. Based on the property's topography, we could not re-design without significant costs, so we chose to remove the muck. Although we incurred that extra expense, our location across from a shopping mall made the property profitable. Remember the earlier secret: you can overcome a lot of mistakes with a good location; but with a bad location, you are finished.

➤   **The native wildlife living on the property.**

On another occasion a group of investors brought me in to consider the purchase of a project that had previously gone bad. The bank had recently foreclosed on the property in question, and now they wanted it sold. The property was zoned for a high-density mixed-use project with multi-family and retail components.

On paper the project looked like it might have some merit. However, a physical inspection of the property unveiled two major issues. First, we found a large wetland area, which significantly reduced the useable acreage of the property. Second, and perhaps even more important, we found an eagle's nest smack in the middle of the property. Being an endangered species, the eagle is protected by the federal government. This nest further reduced the amount of buildable acreage.

The land no longer met our criteria, so we were able to get out of the contract…thanks to the inspection clause. Remember, physical inspections of the property are very important in verifying the facts you have gathered on paper. Hiring a professional engineer, architect, building inspector, contractor, and other professionals are a must. These professionals work for you and will verify exactly what exists in the field.

Power Clause Two-
Contingency of Buyer's Inspection & Approval of the Property's Utilities.

This is another helpful clause to have in your contracts, especially when you're purchasing vacant land. The typical wording is:

Buyer shall have a period of Sixty (Ninety or One Hundred Twenty) days to inspect the utilities to the property to ensure they are in good working order and are suitable in capacity for buyer's intended use.

Failure to include such a clause can be a costly mistake. Here's an example:

The seller of a twenty-acre property represented to the buyers that the water and sewage systems were at the property line along a road. In the purchase contract, the buyers included a clause that the purchase would be subject to their inspection, as well as the availability and location of the utilities. After hiring an engineer and conducting inspections, the buyers discovered that the sewer lines were on the opposite side of the four-lane highway, which they would have to cross to bring the sewer lines to the property. You can imagine the expense that added to the property.

Because the buyers had included the utilities clause, they were able to go back to the seller and ask for more time to analyze this situation.

The seller agreed to a sixty-day extension to the purchase contract as well as a price reduction equivalent to the cost to bring the sewer across the street.

Other Power Clauses to Consider Include:

➢   **Contingency on the approval of the buyer's partners/ board of directors, with a time limit.**

Whenever you're working with an investment partner, you never want to act unilaterally without your partner's input. There- fore, every purchase contract that you present should make the transaction subject to your partner's or board of directors' ap- proval by a certain date. The typical wording is: *"Buyer shall have Thirty days following the satisfaction of the feasibility study to obtain Buyer's Partners or Board of Directors' ap- proval to continue with the proposed purchase of the prop- erty."*

➢   **Inspection of the building, all tenant spaces, tenant leases, and the books for income-producing property.**

Your CPA or financial advisor can review these accounts with you and catch any problems before purchase. The typical word- ing is: *"Buyer shall have Sixty days to inspect the financial records of the property. In the event the buyer does not ap- prove of the inspection, in buyer's sole judgment, buyer may terminate the contract and receive a prompt refund of all de- posits made by buyer."*

➢   **Contingency upon obtaining favorable building permits.**

If you are purchasing vacant land with the intent of building a new structure on it, you want to be sure such a structure is allowed and that you can obtain the correct building permits. Imagine being stuck with a vacant lot that the local government won't let you build on. The usual wording for the clause is: *"The closing of the property will take place X number of days after the buyer obtains a building permit from the appropriate governmental authorities. Buyer agrees to use due diligence in obtaining such permit."*

➢ **Contingency on buyer obtaining a major tenant for the property.**

This is usually stated as *"The buyer shall have X number of days to secure a major tenant for the property."* This ensures that the location will be able to produce a profit.

➢ **Contingency on re-zoning the property.**

This is most important if you are buying and renovating a building. Imagine buying a building with the intent of using it for retail space, only to learn that the zoning board will not allow that kind of business to operate there. This clause is usually presented as, *"The closing of the property will take place X number of days after the buyer obtains a zoning approval from the appropriate governmental authorities for buyer's intended use. Buyer agrees to use due diligence in obtaining such permit."*

A Clause to Beware ~
Contingency of Obtaining Financing Suitable to the Buyer.

Financing contingencies are fine when you're purchasing a single-family home. However, now you are in the real wealth building elite group of professionals, and contingency clauses regarding financing don't work well here. Savvy commercial investors rarely put a financing contingency in any of their contracts.

As you review the contract a buyer presents you, be on the lookout for the following wording:

Buyer shall have a period of One Hundred Twenty days to obtain a first mortgage on the property at an interest rate not to exceed seven percent with an amortization suitable to buyer.

Such a clause should start the red flags flying. Why? That clause reveals to you that the buyer is not very organized and possibly not capable of closing the transaction. Unless you are selling a single-family home, do not accept a financing contingency in any of your offers. If you do, you'll be taking a chance on whether the buyer has the financing in line enough to close the contract. In reality, the buyer should be making the financing arrangements during the inspection period or provide you as the seller some other reassurances from the lender, such as letters of credit.

If you are purchasing a property, this same concept holds true. Asking for a financing contingency will raise red flags with the sellers. They will wonder whether you have enough money to complete the transaction. Additionally, a financing contingency clause puts the buyer in a weak position. You're in the top five percent now. Give yourself the stronger position and do your homework before you get to the table. You will gain credibility with the seller and usually get a better purchase contract if you go into the negotiation with a good handle on your financing.

Here's an example of why you don't want a financing contingency clause:

A partnership was accepting offers for a property they were selling – a national drug store. The financing in the market for this type of property had become over-bought, making it difficult for a lender to place the property in the secondary market. So the partners were receiving offer after offer from interested buyers asking the sellers to either hold purchase money mortgage or accept a purchase contract contingent upon the buyer obtaining acceptable financing. Their answer to both was no. Here's why:

1. When the over-bought situation turned around, they did not want to have tied the partnership up into a worse situation. Having their equity still in the project in the form of a purchase money mortgage would not better their position. Why? With a purchase money mortgage, the seller holds the mortgage and acts much like the bank. The mortgage has a term, an interest rate, and a payment schedule. When banks won't offer the buyer a loan, the seller can opt to offer the loan. Sometimes sellers do this to sell a property that is hard to sell otherwise, and it relieves the owner of the responsibilities of ownership. The owner now becomes the lender, and the new buyer becomes the owner.

2. They were not willing to give up any control of ownership of the property and were experiencing no property management issues. They were not desperate to sell, and they knew they had a great location.

3. They were not willing to tie up the property by entering into a purchase contract while the buyer had loose ends to tie up. They knew they had a great location. The strategy was to let brokers and potential buyers know that they must present offers without a financing contingency. They would agree, however, to the standard inspections and reviews.

Results: Because of the great location, they received a lot of proposals. Their homework, as it related to pricing, paid off. The property sold without the financing contingency, and it sold in the over-bought market described above.

"Clause" Your Own Success

The inspection periods in clauses are designed to protect you, so use them. Be smart and get intimate with the property you are buying during that time period. Learn all you can about the property, from its physical to its financial condition. Hire the right professionals who can supply you with the services and information you need. Even better, go with them to the property to point out your concerns and ask them the questions as you see them. Never forget that *you* are in charge.

Remember that in any purchase contract, the strategy is for the buyer to include as many contingency clauses as the seller will allow, thus protecting the buyer and the buyer's investment and giving the buyer the time to complete the buyer's investment plan. On the other hand, the seller will want to eliminate as many of the contingencies up front as possible, while still selling the property. There is a balancing act involved in this negotiation between buyer and seller.

> Mastering the secrets of this dance will propel you to closing the deal of a lifetime.

Anchoring Ideas ~ An Exercise

Build a Strong
Network &
Win More

With the information in this chapter, you are now a step closer to achieving your dream. However, you still need people to help you. This exercise will help you strengthen your network of contacts.

Take some time to meet with two of the following people:

1. **Bankers -**
    In an earlier exercise you met with bankers. This time go back to the two you liked the most. Introduce yourself again and update them on your plans. Be open, upfront, and honest. These are the people you want to lend you money. They are smart and professional people, so dress appropriately and be sincere. You can get far if you let them know you are just starting out. In most instances they will help you and even point you in helpful directions. Ask them how you should work together from this point forward.

2. **Real Estate Attorneys -**
    Do the same as you did for the bankers.

3. **Mortgage Brokers -**
    Do the same as you did for the bankers.

Next, ask yourself this question: "Where am I going to get the money to finance a project?"

Make a list of everyone you can think of who might help you invest and/ or could give you leads to other lenders or investors. Keep your contact database continually updated by using the latest software that will help you keep your contacts neatly organized.

Chapter Eight –

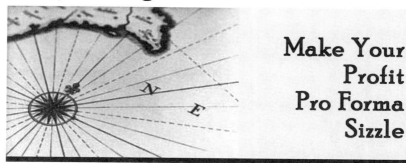

Make Your Profit Pro Forma Sizzle

You have an ideal property. You have an end user in mind. You have open avenues for obtaining financing and locating investors. You have completed the first two stages of the negotiation process Now it's time to create your formal Pro Forma plan, which will specify the potential cash flow and investment returns of the project. Remember, complete your pro forma in the preliminary stage first and then contract for the property. You fine-tune your pro forma plan as you work through the inspection stages set forth in previous chapters.

A great pro forma plan is:

1. Professional
2. Thorough
3. Factual
4. Honest
5. Straightforward

Having all these elements is critical, because your pro forma plan serves many purposes – all of which greatly affect your success.

First, the process of finalizing the pro forma plan forces you to think through the proposed investment in even greater detail than before. You will see all the perspectives, all the potential questions for your investors, and all the steps you need to take to complete your plan.

Second, your pro forma plan assists you in the management of your investment. It will be your guide, if you will, a point of reference that shows your progress and how well you did.

Finally, your pro forma plan is your vehicle for communicating your ideas to your investors. When your investors see your ideas in writing, with pictures, graphs, and all the other materials, they will have a better concept of your project. Visually, your ideas come alive.

Showing your plan to investors is much more effective than simply telling them about it. Why? It's biological. The human eye contains many nerve and communications connections that go directly to the brain. The human ear contains a fewer number of these connections. While it would be ideal to have your investors see the plan, smell it, feel it, taste it, and hear it, that's not realistic. Since we usually only have one choice in how we communicate our ideas to others, "sight" is the hands-down winner in terms of comprehension and retention every time.

Planning Makes Perfect

In order to present a professional plan, you must do your fair share of homework. Realize that you're not being timed when it comes to preparing your plan, nor are you in a race. So take your time with the process. Over half of all real estate projects fail to meet the investors' requirements because people didn't take their time while constructing their pro forma plan, resulting in overlooked information and careless mistakes. Don't fall into this trap.

Your pro forma plan will be the sole evaluation tool your investors and lenders use. When your plan is thorough, complete, and accurate, you enable your investors to make quick and easy decisions.

As investors review your plan, they are looking for some key items. They want to be certain that:

1. **The information contained in the plan is accurate, based on facts and not based on theory or opinion.**
    Any lender or investor(s) that you approach with your plan will test your assumptions and try to poke holes in your projections. Be prepared for this and realize that it's not a direct assault. They are simply doing their jobs. If you have not done your homework and your plan fails the test, you will lose. That's why taking your time and double checking your own findings are so important. Test your plan. Would you invest in your project?

    It's very common for lenders and/or investors to ask you point blank, *"Would you invest your own money into this and why?"* Should this happen to you, remember that the key part of the question is the "why." Justify your actions and back them up with *facts*.

2. **The plan is consistent.**

   Bankers and investors use a set "rule of thumb" when analyzing and comparing proposals. They look at proposals all day long and compare one to the other. As a result, they know what realistic projections should look like. If you don't know what you are talking about, don't "fudge it." Rest assured that your investors will know the answer, and if you exaggerate your findings or make unrealistic claims, you'll lose credibility instantly. Always find the correct information prior to presenting your plan.

3. **The information provides lenders and investors their required investment returns versus risk.**

   Every lender and investor has a risk tolerance. Regardless of how well your plan matches their needs, if it is beyond their acceptable level of risk, they will reject it. Now, this does not mean that you should alter your figures just to suit their requirements. Investors know what a typical return on investment should look like. If your figures are off, they'll spot it in a minute. For example, if the going rate of return for Certificates of Deposit, a very safe investment held by a banking institution, is five percent, then to request a five percent return of capital for your investors would be foolish. If you do find a lender who would agree to this, then run away as fast as possible, because the lender or investor is being unrealistic and you will have problems with them down the line.

4. **The plan is tailored for your investors.**

   Know the kinds of investments and returns your investors expect. By questioning your investors and listening to their responses you will learn the key to their investment criteria. For example, if a particular investor prefers to invest in vacant land, then you probably won't receive a favorable response for a presentation regarding an office building. Save yourself the time and trouble by only presenting investors with the kinds of investments they like.

   However, this does not mean that you want to ignore potential investors just because they may have rejected a particular project in the past. Keep yourself in the front of the investors' minds by contacting them and casually letting them know what you have to offer. You could say, "I know this might not be of interest to you, but I thought you might want to have the opportunity to say 'no' to this property before I present it to others." That soft approach may shock you with the results. You could get a response like, "Yes. You are right, but thanks for thinking of me," or "Well, I am not sure. Can you tell me more about this opportunity?" Or better yet, "I am not interested, but I know someone who might be. Let me introduce you to them." Knowing your investors as well as you know your property will reap great rewards for you.

As you offer investment opportunities to various investors, confer with your attorney so you can be sure that you are complying with your state's rules and regulations for offering investments to individuals. The Federal limit is one hundred accredited individuals. "Accredited" means the individual has a net worth equal to or greater than $1,000,000. Spend the $150 or so for a one-hour meeting with your attorney. He or she can assist your fundraising efforts. Your attorney may even know of other individuals interested in investing in your proposal. Your goal is to stay within the guidelines of exemptions from registering the proposal as provided under the Securities and Exchange Act. This involves the size of your investment and the type of investor you are contacting.

Appeal to Your Potential Investors

Each experienced investor reads the pro forma proposal in a similar manner. Although you shouldn't turn away a novice investor, a more experienced investor will be the most helpful to you and may even point out potential problems with your plan. Should this happen, stay open-minded and listen to their comments. They are giving you valuable free advice that will add to your future success.

Whether you're preparing a pro forma or evaluating one, be sure to go over it with the following guidelines in mind.

How to Produce a Winning Plan:

➤ 1. **Define the project?**

Everyone has his or her preferred type of real estate investment. Some people prefer to only invest in office complexes, while others feel safer investing in vacant land. Many others shift their investment preferences based on their current portfolio mix or need. Regardless of the investment type, experienced investors will always look at whether the specified market is in an upswing or downswing.

☑ Remember, each segment of the market has its cycle (as discussed previously in chapter four).
Where is your project in the cycle?

(Tip: It's much easier and more advantageous to buy on the beginning of the upswing of any cycle.)

☑ Has the project been done before? Are the investors familiar with the project type?

☑ Will the investors think the project makes sense?
Do the project costs fit with the demographics of the area? Are the market rents consistent with the demographics of its location?

☑ Is the project pioneering (as discussed previously in chapter four)? Is the project ahead of the demographic base? How much time will it take the demographic growth to reach the property?

(Note: The longer the time, the greater change you'll see in the risk and the returns.)

Check the market area and then fine-tune the property accordingly. Regardless of the remainder of the plan, if the proposal doesn't fit this first criterion, the investors will pass.

➤ 2. **What are the terms of the investment opportunity?**

The key issue here is how the project will be funded. Investors are mainly concerned with the following:

☑ **Debt** – If there is too much debt on the project, the risk of failure may increase. Investors may be willing to invest more in order to reduce the amount of debt and risk. Time and tenant delays equate to loss of income

and could significantly impact a highly leveraged
property.

☑ **Equity** – How much equity is required and when is it
due? Have you eliminated much of the upfront risk in
the project before most of the equity is required
and becomes at risk? How much of the project are the
investors getting of the total project versus the amount
of equity required? Does 100% of the equity equal 100%
of the project? Satisfy your investors. The story in the
introduction is a great reference for investor needs.

☑ **Risk** – Does the project make sense?
(Review chapter five.)

☑ **Profit potential** – Are your projections realistic and
worthwhile?

☑ **Minimum investment** – How much will each investor
have to put up? For example you may be looking for
five investors to fund $25,000 each for a total equity
requirement of $125,000.

☑ **Number of investors** – How many people will be
involved and who are they? Do they know any of the
other investors? And if there is a problem, how will
everyone get through it?

☑ **Exit strategy** – What are the long-term projections for
how and when everyone will get their return?

All of the above items are connected and factor into the analysis of the
proposal. The key point for you to remember is to be fair and exact in
your presentation.

➤3.   **What are the cash flow projections?**

☑ What do the numbers look like? Figure 8a is an example of a pro forma cash flow statement. An investor
will always look at the potential downside. They want
to determine how quickly they could recover if the
project should go bad and force them to sell. How
quickly could they liquidate and what would they
receive?

Figure 8a – Preliminary Cash Flow Projection

Preliminary Cash Flow Projection

PARTENERSHIP NAME:_____

PROJECT: _____ START DATE : _____

LOCATION:_____ COMPLETION DATE:_____

CASH FLOW	BUDGET	TOTAL FORECAST	MONTH					
			1	2	3	4	5	6
SOURCES								
Seed Capital								
Equity From Partners								
Development Loan								
Sales Proceeds								
Less: Closing Costs								
Plus: Legal Costs								
Total Sources								
REQUIREMENTS								
Development Costs:								
Land Cost								
Hard Cost								
TIs & Leasing Commissions								
Soft Costs								
Total Development Cost								
Administrative Expenses								
Repayment of Development Loan								
Return of Equity								
Return of Seed Capital								
Total Requirements								
Net Change								
Distribution to Seed Capital								
Distribution to Partners								
Total								

☑ What is the added value of the project based on the cash flow projections the investor thinks are attainable? This determines the project's current potential for the investor. If your numbers are off or overstated, the experienced investors will discount the figures and calculate the project to their liking.

☑ A potential investor will also always look to the value added in the equity investment. Remember that you add value to the project as well. Without you, the work can't get done. That translates to no investment opportunity for the investor.

➤4.   **Who is involved in the project?**

☑ The reputation of you and your team members is what's studied here. Do you and your team members have a track record for getting things done or have you been involved in this type of investment before? If your answer is no, you should find someone who has that reputation, even if you have to give them some of the ownership for the expertise. In the formation of your ownership entity, use partners to boost your credibility. Your real estate attorney is good to have as an advisor and can bring credibility to the project. Additionally, accountants, bankers, engineers, architects, and other real estate brokers are all good sources to bring credibility to your plan. This is a guaranteed attraction to any investor.

➤5.   **What makes this investment better than the hundreds of others an investor sees every day?**

☑ What is your proposal's competitive advantage? Is there something your property offers that no other available property does? Maybe it's a better location or a better rent potential. Properties that are better than the competition possess the potential to attract capital. Remember, you can overcome a lot with a great location, but you are finished with a bad location.

If your plan answers the above concerns adequately, then you are on your way to a successful investment.

Outline of a Great Pro Forma Proposal

Your creativity will help you prepare a winning finalized pro forma plan. Regardless of how creative you are remember to be very business-like and professional. The exact organization of your data into the plan is something that we do not discuss here because it is extremely personal to the individual and the individual proposal.

To create a great pro forma proposal, you need to get intimate with your plan. If you are using a fill-in-the-blank form, you will not be able to customize the plan or get intimate with it. Further, if you are not intimate with the plan, you will not be able to sell it to your investors. The goal is for you to succeed. Have confidence; you can create a great plan. By generating your own plan you will easily sell it to your investors.

With that said, there are certain ideas that are common to most proposals, and you will find a good number of those listed below. Remember, the purpose of your plan is to see where you are going and to raise the required funds for your project.

Your plan should include the following:
1. Table of contents.
2. Introduction. Briefly, in no more than one typewritten page, describe the investment opportunity. The description should include:
   A. A physical description of the property.
   B. A brief history of the market data that makes this property appealing over its competitors.
   C. Detail of the investment opportunity, its profit potential, and why.
3. Name of the property or proposed project.
4. Complete aerial photographs of the property or an artist's rendering of the proposed project.
5. Investment goal. Examples include:
   A. How you can maximize the investment returns by selling the property within a specific time period for _____ dollars.
   B. How you can minimize the investment risk by

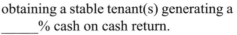

obtaining a stable tenant(s) generating a
_____% cash on cash return.

6.   Competition and market studies.

7.   Principals of the project and brief summary of their
      qualifications (this is the "who's involved" part).

8.   Financial information.

    A.   Equity required

    B.   Debt structure

    C.   Pro forma

    D.   Risk analysis: Define the risk in the project as
      you see it. For example as shown in Figure 8b,
      the risk is stated that if we cannot sell the
      property and obtain the sales price, then are
      we comfortable with holding the property for
      the thirteen percent cash on cash return it
      generates until we can sell the property.

9.   Overview of the investment structure and the opportu-
      nity. Some important items for this section include:

    A.   The amount of money required per each
      investor

    B.   The number of investment units available (the
      maximum number of investors allowed)

    C.   The due date for the investment capital

10.   An investment timeline and a detailed exit strategy.
      Knowing how long their money is going to be invested
      is critical to each investor as they calculate their poten-
      tial returns.

11.   List of advantages to investors. Examples include:

    A.   The ability to leave something to their heirs

    B.   The ability to increase their investor liquidity
      by obtaining a stabilized base rent with a credit
      tenant

    C.   The ability to sell the property quickly for
      $_____

In some cases you can provide investors with a one-page summary of
the final plan in order to test their interest in receiving the more detailed
plan.

Figure 8b - Risk Analysis

Preliminary Pro Forma

Project: A Single Tenant Retail

Budget Item	Cost
1. Property Price	$850,000
2. Property Development	65,000
3. Vertical Construction Shell with Tenant Specifications	580,000
4. Parking	70,000
5. Architect	10,000
6. Engineer	15,000
7. Permits and approval fees	68,000
8. Testing and Inspections	6,000
9. Landscaping	14,000
10. Signage-----in shell number	0
11. Surveying	3,000
12. Exterior lighting-----in shell	0
13. Tenant Improvements-----in shell	0
14. Leasing and RE Commissions	78,000
15. Closing and title fees	13,200
16. Legal	7,000
17. Financing Fees	13,875
18. Interest	38,000
19. Contingency 5%	27,000
20. Real Estate Taxes-construction	5,000
A. Total Project Cost	**$1,863,075**
21. Gross potential rents 11,000sf Tenant 1-Single Tenant Tenant 2	$203,500
22. Vacancy Factor	0
23. Effective Gross Rent	203,500
24. Debt Service	165,756
25. Net Income From Operations	**37,743**
26. Equity Required	**300,000**
27. Cash on Cash Return	**13%**

Assumptions

Loan Amount	1,563,075
Interest Rate	8.75%
Debt Service	165,756
Rental Rate Year One	18.50
Rental Rate Annual Escalations.	2%
Operating Expense Pass Through Tenant	

Exit Strategy

Potential Buyers will pay $2,400,000. Sell at start of lease.

Hint: Are buyers waiting in line to purchase or are they non-existent?

Total Potential Return

$2,400,000 less $1,863,075, equals approximately $500,000 less some closing expense

170% return on investment of $300,000.00

If no, hold at 13% Cash on Cash Return

Hint: Are we comfortable holding the property at 13% Cash on Cash it generates until we sell?

How does this compare to other safer investments such as T-Bills or CDs?

Proceed

How to Make a Gazillion Dollars

Always finalize an exit strategy before you make a proposal for or purchase any property. In fact, a large portion of your investment proposal should be geared toward the end. How are you going to make that big hit? If you have followed the strategies in this book, you have seen something in the property that others have not. Therefore, you have created hidden value in the property, and your plan should now be to tap that hidden value.

Other long-term investors, such as pension funds, some real estate investment trusts, or even extremely wealthy individuals, might be interested in purchasing your new property. The return these types of investors are looking for is much smaller than the money you want to make. These long-term investors aren't willing to spend their time creating the project. They are willing to take smaller returns, less risk, and simply let their money work. By seeing what others can't, taking action, and exerting the effort, you can generate large sums of money.

For example, one of our partnerships purchased an old bowling alley situated on a two-acre lot. This high-quality location was a far corner at a major intersection. The purchase price was $1,000,000. **(Note: Don't become frustrated with that big number. You'll soon see how the structure of this transaction would get any seasoned investor drooling to get a piece of this opportunity.)**
Our pro forma plan showed the creation of two separate parcels. Market studies showed the need for a gas station, and zoning allowed for it. It also showed the need for a drug store chain. With that information, we decided to split the property into two separate parcels. Selling the first parcel to a national oil company would net almost $600,000. This sale would leave us about $400,000 in our cost basis in the remainder of the property. Our total cost in the project would be about $2,150,000, including money for the renovations.

In our plan, we networked with a bank that would loan us about $1,850,000 to cover all the costs, including demolishing the existing structure and making the necessary improvements. Our market studies suggested that we could sell the new structure on the second lot with a tenant in place for approximately $2,350,000. The project required $300,000 in equity. Upon successful execution of the plan we stood to earn a return of about 200%. Now, what investor wouldn't want to be a part of that return?

Here's a breakdown of the detailed math: The sales prices of $2,350,000 plus $600,000 equals $2,950,000. Subtract from that our total project cost of $2,150,000, and the result is $800,000. From that figure we deduct our real estate commissions and closing costs, which leaves about $600,000 in profit. Not a bad proposition by any means.

By clearly defining our exit strategy, we showed the complete process from beginning to the end. Any investor could see the huge return of their money.

Keep your plan detailed to the end and you will notice more than an 80% in potential investors responding with a resounding "Yes!"

With this strategy, your income will skyrocket.

Chapter Eight:
Anchoring Ideas ~ An Exercise

Create a
Professional
Proposal

You have what it takes to become a member of the elite – the top five percent of the real wealth builders. Now is where patience, persistence, focus, and continued action come into play. Use the tools in this book to propel you further. You will attain what you desire.

Your assignment:

Prepare a preliminary your pro forma plan on a property you are considering for investment. Gather all the information you need and commence the writing process. If you uncover areas where you are lacking information, go to the source and gather what you need. Keep your plan as thorough, factual, professional, and complete as possible. Have a seasoned investor look over your plan and listen to the feedback you receive.

This will be your best learning experience.

Chapter Nine ~

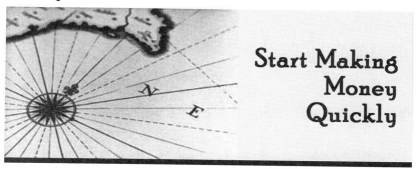

Start Making Money Quickly

Congratulations on completing the book and the exercises. You now have the tools you need to build significant wealth in commercial real estate. Go out and do it. Give your new real estate endeavor 110%, because when you do, you will gain great confidence and know that you can succeed at this adventure. Failure to devote 110% will result in the age-old question "what if ?" You are worth much more than that.

As you employ the philosophies and principles in this book and progress in your real estate wealth-building venture, you will see your life change in many ways. An evolution will occur in the way you think and communicate to the way you plan, prepare, and accumulate large sums of spendable cash. The more you change what you are doing, the greater the results you will receive. Your new outlook and philosophies will carry through to other areas of your life, enabling you to reach personal goals as well.

As your coach throughout the past eight chapters, I have complete faith in you and your abilities. You will be completely successful as long as you believe in yourself. While starting on any new endeavor may seem scary at first, your inner belief in your own future and your own success will continually urge you forward.

Use all the tools provided to you and refer back to this book as needed. Techniques and secrets that you may have missed the first or even second time will gradually reveal themselves to you. As you master the strategies discussed, your bank account will swell. You'll be amazed at how quickly the implementation of powerful information can change your life.

Generate a Significant Profit

You can make a significant profit very quickly without investing any of your own money and without a real estate license, if you choose. Just follow through with the lessons you've learned namely:

1. Enthusiastically incorporate a new way of living your life. Realize that the actions you take or don't take are a direct link to the results you achieve. Therefore, if you don't like the results, change the actions.

2. Know the value of your time. You can spend your time however you like, but realize that time is money. So if you want to spend your time watching television, that's your choice. Just be aware that you'll never regain that time or be able to put it towards accomplishing goals in your life.

3. Obtain all the knowledge you can. Those who are really serious about changing their life educate themselves continually. For you this may mean attending real estate school and obtaining your real estate license. As stated earlier, you don't need your real estate license to build your wealth, but obtaining your license will add to your knowledge bank immediately.

4. Network easily and effectively. No person can do everything alone. We all need help from competent people in order to reach our goals. Align yourself with the most reputable professionals in your area and work to help each other succeed.

5. Invest in yourself. Purchase a software-mapping program. The right tools will help you reach your goals faster. Invest in yourself by expanding your technology. A good mapping program will save you much time and make your job easier and more enjoyable.

6. Drive your territory and note important findings on the map. The more you know about your territory, the better real estate decisions you'll be able to make. Driving your territory is an important part of your job, so always take this task seriously.

7. Identify high-quality properties in your area. Know what's needed in your area as well as what town or county improvements are in the works. When you can see something in the property that no one else can see, you'll have the potential for significant profit.

8. Identify the end user. Know the demographics of your area as well as the land layout. Having a goal for the property in mind will greatly increase its profitability.

9. Prepare a preliminary pro forma projection for the property. Be thorough as you gather your information. Your attention to detail at this stage will pay off in the long run.

10. Get the property under contract. Work your network for attorneys and potential investors. Set up investor meetings, and then negotiate for the best deal for all parties.

11. Finalize your pro forma presentation. Be professional, factual, and honest about every detail. Show that you know what will work for this property and that you are just the person to get the job done.

12. Meet with potential investors and raise the money. Tailor the presentation to your investors and make your investment opportunity irresistible.

13. Enthusiastically believe in your project. Without a strong personal belief in the project, you'll have a hard time convincing others to believe in it. Spend time in thoughtful preparation and planning so you can uncover all the positive and negative aspects of the project. Work to reverse the negatives and then build upon the positives. People will believe in you if you believe in yourself.

14. Close the transaction. Providing that you followed all the steps precisely and professionally, closing will be the easy part. Some hard work upfront delivers a huge payoff in the end.

15. Collect a huge check with your superior exit strategy. There's no limit to the money you can earn. Having a long-term mentality is the key to building real wealth that will last a lifetime.

It All Starts With You

Only you can determine your success in commercial real estate. Accept the belief that you can do it. Don't settle for anything less. Follow the lessons in this book and you will be well on your way to creating the lifestyle you want. Before you know it, brokers will be coming to *you* with proposals.

Keep to the basics when evaluating any property. Remember the importance of location, and watch your income skyrocket. It can happen and will happen if you start now. Plan for your success today and follow through to the finish. You are the only obstacle to your success. Change your old habits, strengthen your beliefs, and decide on what you want.

With such a mindset, you will succeed.

Chapter Nine:
Anchoring Ideas ~ An Exercise

Stake Your Claim

Your final assignment is to actually put the techniques you learned in this book to use.

1. Reread any sections or chapters that you need clarification on.

2. If you skipped any of the previous exercises, go back and complete them in sequential order. Remember, each exercise and habit builds upon the previous one.

3. Build the necessary relationships, scout your territory, stick to the facts, and believe in your ability to master this program.

So take the first important step to your future – to your victory in commercial real estate.

Don't Procrastinate.
Start Today.

You *Can* Do This!

Accredited Individuals – People who have a net worth in excess of $1,000,000.

Acre – A way to measure land. One acre equals 43,560 square feet.

Aerial Photograph – A picture of the property taken from the air, usually in an airplane or helicopter.

Agricultural Zoning – Land designated for agricultural purposes only.

Base Value – The value of the property less the value of the land. Base value is calculated at the time of purchase or if the project is new construction then at the time of construction.

Below Market Pricing – A property that is priced less than the other comparable properties currently available for sale in a given area.

Building and Zoning Department – The branch of government that enforces the building and zoning regulations for a particular municipality. Their offices are usually located in the complex that houses all other government offices for the municipality. Their telephone number is in the local phone book under "government offices."

Building Inspection – An examination of the property, usually performed by a person referred to as an "inspector" and whom the building department employs.

Building Permits – Rights issued by the building department to build to the specifications provided on the building plans as submitted to the building department.

Cash on Cash Return – The amount of cash returned on your cash invested.

$$\frac{\text{Net Income}}{\text{Equity}} = \text{Cash on Cash Return}$$

Commercial Zoning – A property that can be used for business uses.

Comparable Sales – Prior sales of similar properties used for determining a particular property's value.

Competition – The act of one business taking customers from another business. This usually happens when two businesses offering the same product or service are located too close to one another.

Condemnation Proceedings – The procedures taken by a governing body, afforded to them by law, to purchase land from the private sector for various uses.

Contingency – Subject to an unforeseen event.

Conventional Financing – A loan given for a project from a mainstream lender such as a bank or insurance company.

Debt – The amount of money owed a lender for a project. Payback terms include an interest rate, an amortization schedule, and a timeframe to pay back the loan.

Egress – The ability to exit the property.

End User – The consumer who will ultimately use the property.

Environmental Studies – Studies performed to examine the condition of the property to uncover any hazardous wastes such as petroleum or asbestos, and to identify any protected species of animal or plant on a given property.

Equity – The amount of money and value in a project above the debt.

Far Corner – The corner past the traffic control device at an intersection.

Feasibility Study – An evaluation to determine the achievability of a project.

Geotechnical Engineer – A professional versed in studying the earth's soil and subsurface conditions.

Ingress – The ability to enter the property.

Inspection Period – The timeframe allotted in a purchase contract for examining all aspects of the property.

Land Use Plan – A plan developed by the governing body that determines the use of certain lands. This plan is used in determining how the municipality will develop.

Macro – Large-scale; comprehensive.

Muck – The decayed waste of tree leaves and other natural wastes.

Multi-Family Zoned – Property that can be used for many housing units such as an apartment complex.

Near Corner – The corner prior to the traffic control device at an intersection.

Objective Thinker – A person who bases decisions strictly on the facts and keeps emotions out.

Opportunity Loss – The perceived value of the investment returns lost by not investing.

Preferred Return – The income received first from an investment.

Preliminary Pro Forma – A rough draft of the costs and income potential in the transaction. A form that assumes certain criteria to decide the viability of the project.

Pro Forma – A form specifying the potential cash flow and investment returns of a particular project. The form also contains a list of assumptions made while creating the pro forma.

Property Appraiser's Office – The branch of government that sets the valuation of real estate for the purposes of collecting real estate taxes. The taxes are usually calculated based on a formula as applied to the value of real estate. Their offices are usually located in the complex that houses all other government offices for the municipality. Their telephone number is in the local phone book under "government offices."

Purchase Money Mortgage – A loan given for a project from the seller of the property.

Raw Land – Vacant land.

Real Estate Commission – The payment a licensed real estate broker receives for the services of selling a real estate property. Payment is only received if and when the property sells.

Return On Investment – The amount of money received on the actual money used for the venture.

Risk – Any chance or possibility of loss. Risk is determined by the quality of the facts regarding the investment opportunity compared to a safer investment.

Signatures – The signing of names on a debt instrument and promissory note indicating the party's pledge to pay back the debt.

Single-Family Zoned – Property that can be used for one family dwelling unit only.

Soil Borings – Samples of the earth's soil and subsurface condition.

Subjective Thinker – A person who bases decisions on their emotions.

Under Contract – The term used to describe when a property contains an active purchase and sale agreement.

Unlimited Access Highway – A roadway that has an unlimited amount of entry and exit points.

Vacant Land – Land that is without any structure on it.

About the Author

Al Auger is a 22-year veteran of the commercial real estate industry. In addition to being a Licenced Real Estate Broker, Investment Partner, and Real Estate Developer, he is also a successful Business Strategist.

Mr. Auger's services have benefited national companies such as Home Depot, Burger King, Eckerd's Drugs, Costco Wholesale Club, Auto Nation USA, Golden Corral, Walgreen's Drugs, Sun Trust Bank, Subway, and many others. Clients universally praise the practical advice and detail-oriented approach Mr. Auger consistently displays.

In addition to writing *Pure Profits*, Mr. Auger is an expert source and writes articles for national publications such as *Money 'N Profits, Sales & Marketing Excellence, Bull and Bear Financial, Commercial Mortgage Insight, The Real Estate Professional, International Real Estate Digest,* and many others.

Al currently lives in Orlando with his wife and son.

Contact Information:
Phone: (407) 304-4714